African Americans in the Jazz Age

The African American History Series

Series Editors:
Jacqueline M. Moore, Austin College
Nina Mjagkij, Ball State University

Traditionally, history books tend to fall into two categories: books academics write for each other, and books written for popular audiences. Historians often claim that man of the popular authors do not have the proper training to interpret and evaluate the historical evidence. Yet, popular audiences complain that most historical monographs are inaccessible because they are too narrow in scope or lack an engaging style. This series, which will take both chronological and thematic approaches to topics and individuals crucial to an understanding of the African American experience, is an attempt to address that problem. The books in this series, in lively prose by established scholars, are aimed primarily at nonspecialists. They focus on topics in African American history that have broad significance and place them in their historical context. While presenting sophisticated interpretations based on primary sources and the latest scholarship, the authors tell their stories in a succinct manner, avoiding jargon and obscure language. They include selected documents that allow readers to judge the evidence for themselves and to evaluate the authors' conclusions. Bridging the gap between popular and academic history, these books bring the African American story to life.

Volumes Published

Booker T. Washington, W.E.B. DuBois, and the Struggle for Racial Uplift
Jacqueline M. Moore

Slavery in Colonial America, 1619–1776
Betty Wood

African Americans in the Jazz Age
A Decade of Struggle and Promise
Mark Robert Schneider

African Americans in the Jazz Age

A Decade of Struggle and Promise

Mark Robert Schneider

ROWMAN & LITTLEFIELD PUBLISHERS, INC.
Lanham • Boulder • New York • Toronto • Oxford

ROWMAN & LITTLEFIELD PUBLISHERS, INC.

Published in the United States of America
by Rowman & Littlefield Publishers, Inc.
A wholly owned subsidary of The Rowman & Littlefield Publishing Group, Inc.
4501 Forbes Boulevard, Suite 200, Lanham, Maryland 20706
www.rowmanlittlefield.com

PO Box 317
Oxford
OX2 9RU, UK

British Library Cataloguing in Publication Information Available

Library of Congress Cataloging-in-Publication Data

Schneider, Mark R. (Mark Robert), 1948–
    African Americans in the Jazz Age : a decade of struggle and promise / Mark Robert
Schneider.
        p.   cm. — (The African American history series)
    Includes bibliographical references and index.
    ISBN-13: 978-0-7425-4416-1 (cloth : alk. paper)
    ISBN-10: 0-7425-4416-8 (cloth : alk. paper)
    ISBN-13: 978-0-7425-4417-8 (pbk. : alk. paper)
    ISBN-10: 0-7425-4417-6 (pbk. : alk. paper)
    1. African Americans—History—1877–1964.   2. African Americans—Social
condition—To 1964.   3. African Americans—Civil rights—History—20th century.
4. United States—Race relations—History—20th century.   5. United States—
History—1919–1933.   I. Title.   II. Series: African American history series
(Lanham, Md.)

E185.6.S36   2006
973'.0496073—dc22   2006001096

Printed in the United States of America

♾ ™ The paper used in this publication meets the minimum requirements of American
National Standard for Information Sciences—Permanence of Paper for Printed Library
Materials, ANSI/NISO Z39.48-1992.

Contents

Credits

Chronology

November 11, 1918
  Armistice Ends World War

1919

February
  African American veterans parade in New York City
  W. E. B. DuBois opens Pan-African Congress in Paris

March
  Commission on Interracial Cooperation launched
  Antilynching conference convenes in New York City
  Whites attack black citizens in Charleston, South Carolina, beginning a
    "Red Summer" of violence

July
  White violence meets black resistance at Longview, Texas, Washington,
    D.C., and Chicago

September
  More rioting at Chattanooga, Tennessee, and Omaha, Nebraska
  Claude McKay's "If We Must Die" published

October
  Whites attack black cotton growers in Phillips County, Arkansas

1920

February
  Lexington, Kentucky, militia fires into would-be lynch mob

June
  Lynch mob kills three African Americans at Duluth, Minnesota

August
  Marcus Garvey's Universal Negro Improvement Association opens New
    York convention
  Okeh Record Company launches Race Records

November
  African American women vote for first time
  Whites burn Ocoee, Florida
  James Weldon Johnson appointed first African American executive secre-
    tary of NAACP
  Rube Foster forms National Negro Baseball League

1921

January
  Henry Lowry burned at the stake in Tennessee

February
  Williams farm murders revealed in Georgia

May
  Tulsa, Oklahoma, race riot

August
  Second Pan-African Congress
  National Negro Insurance Association formed
  "Shuffle Along," all-black musical, staged on Broadway

1922

  Mary B. Talbert launches Antilynching Crusaders
  Three African Americans burned at stake in Kirvin, Texas
  Dyer Antilynching bill fails in the U.S. Senate
  Claude McKay's *Harlem Shadows* published

1923

January
  Rosewood, Florida, burned

February

U.S. Supreme Court overturns convictions of Arkansas defendants in
Moore v. Dempsey

May

Marcus Garvey tried for conspiracy

July

Ku Klux Klan parades at Negro Veterans' Hospital
Jean Toomer's *Cane* published

1924

February

African American leaders present clemency petition for participants in
1917 Houston mutiny to President Calvin Coolidge

July

Dr. Lawrence A. Nixon denied ballot in Texas Democratic primary
Mary McLeod Bethune elected president of National Association of
Colored Women's Clubs
Louis Armstrong leaves New Orleans to join King Oliver's band in
Chicago
Kansas City Monarchs win first Negro League baseball championship
Jessie Redmon Fauset's *There Is Confusion* published

1925

February

Fisk University students at Nashville, Tennessee, strike

May

National Urban League's *Opportunity* magazine literary awards banquet

August

A. Philip Randolph takes over campaign to organize Brotherhood of
Sleeping Car Porters Union
Ku Klux Klan marches in Washington

September

White mob attacks home of Dr. Ossian Sweet in Detroit
The New Negro, edited by Alain Locke, published
Langston Hughes's *Weary Blues* published
Paul Robeson stars in play *The Emperor Jones*

1926

March
> Survey Graphic special edition "Harlem: Mecca of the New Negro" published

October
> Three members of Lowman family lynched at Aiken, South Carolina

1927

> Mississippi River flood
> Gary, Indiana, school segregation battle
> Marcus Garvey deported to Jamaica

November
> Huge Harlem funeral for singer Florence Mills

1928

November
> Chicago alderman Oscar De Priest elected to U.S. Congress

1929

October
> Stock market crash ends "Roaring Twenties"

INTRODUCTION

~

What the World War Wrought

The Great War that had raged in Europe between August 1914 and November 1918 had far-reaching social effects all over the world. Attitudes toward government and society changed in Europe, America, the colonial world, and among African Americans in the United States. In America, the war encouraged a migration of black people from the South, mobilized hundreds of thousands of black men as soldiers, and inspired a struggle for democracy at home. The end of the war began the end of the Jim Crow system of segregation and disfranchisement. A "New Negro" emerged on the battlefields of Europe, determined to make America safe for democracy. It would take another world war and twenty more years of struggle to complete the process, but the outline of what was to come began with World War I.

This book tells the story of African Americans in the eleven years after the war. The 1920s were marked by economic growth, consumerism, retreat from international affairs, political conservatism, gains in women's rights, and the development of mass culture. The economic growth and exuberance of the time came to an end with the stock market crash of October 1929, ushering in a lean decade of depression. Novelist F. Scott Fitzgerald called the 1920s the "Jazz Age," marking the first time that an African American contribution to the national culture had defined an era. Many African Americans enjoyed the good times just as much as whites, but they also nurtured the dream of achieving equal citizenship. During the 1920s, African Americans built new communities, new institutions, and a new culture that would contribute to the overthrow of Jim Crow in the years following World War II.

In the decades before World War I, race relations had steadily worsened in the United States. With the removal of federal troops from the South in

1

1877, the Southern states passed laws mandating the segregation and disfranchisement of black voters. African Americans who hoped to become independent landowners were often forced into tenant farming or sharecropping, types of labor that left them economically dependent on whites. Those who protested faced beating or lynching. Recognizing that their former Northern friends were doing nothing to challenge this new arrangement, many African Americans concluded that they could make little immediate progress. From 1895 until his death in 1915, Booker T. Washington, the main spokesperson for black America, argued that racial advancement had to be slow, focused on vocational education and economic progress. Washington urged black people to accommodate, rather than confront, white prejudices. In the South, where 90 percent of African Americans lived, white politicians expressed crude racism toward black people. Even progressive politicians in the North commonly held reactionary views on race relations.

The start of World War I in Europe in August of 1914 had a tremendous effect on African Americans. Before the United States entered the war in April 1917, the industrial North began to produce arms and supplies for export to the Allies, boosting the demand for factory labor. At the same time, the war cut off the supply of European immigrants, who could no longer cross the ocean. Then the boll weevil ate up the cotton, making survival hard for anyone growing that cash crop. African Americans were pushed out of the rural South by continuing lack of freedom and economic hardship and pulled toward the industrial North by the promise that both problems would be ameliorated there. The Great Migration, the single largest population movement in the history of black America, had begun.

A second change in race relations came with American entry into the war in April 1917. Almost four hundred thousand black men joined the army. Unlike during the Civil War, many black soldiers would serve under the command of African American officers. While most black soldiers were assigned to noncombat duties, some regiments served courageously at the front, smashing through enemy resistance and reaching the Rhine ahead of white units. French villagers recognized their bravery and were grateful. The experience showed black soldiers that they could defeat white men in battle, and it strengthened their confidence and resolve.

Yet, the army remained a racist institution. Black men served in segregated units, and African American officers trained at a segregated camp in Des Moines, Iowa. The generals put black troops under French command, wanting nothing to do with them, and advised French officers to treat the African Americans coldly. Most black soldiers experienced insult and betrayal when they came into contact with whites, and there were instances of unprovoked assaults on black "doughboys" by their white comrades. At home, many African Americans regarded the war as a meaningless struggle among colonial powers that promised them nothing but death. Draft boards turned down legitimate requests for deferment. Lynching continued, just as it had before the war. The whole experience of fighting and dying for other people's freedom, when it was denied to them at home, made black Americans furious.

Lastly, African Americans could see that World War I had touched off an international cry for freedom from foreign domination. In declaring war, President Woodrow Wilson had promised to "make the world safe for democracy." During the conflict, his Fourteen Points emphasized the creation of new European nations. When the war ended on November 11, 1918, Poland, Czechoslovakia, Hungary, Yugoslavia, and Ireland shook off imperial control. Moreover, Africans and Indians, who had also fought in the war, began to demand freedom from colonial oppression. Many African Americans felt themselves to be part of this international movement.

The almost four hundred thousand black men who had served in the army had left a country that expected them to show deference to whites at every juncture. On the street, they were supposed to get out of white people's way. At work, they were supposed to serve, fetch, and carry. In politics, they were to do as they were told. After the war, African Americans had had enough of this treatment. The "New Negroes" were not afraid; they were proud of their heritage, and they were determined to enjoy the benefits of full American citizenship.

This book shows how they did that. Each chapter discusses a different aspect of the African American experience during the Jazz Age. In the 1920s, black Americans fought back against white violence, moved to the North, built new institutions, fought for civil rights, and showed black pride through a cultural renaissance.

Following the war, black men fought back when whites attacked them, turning some Northern and border communities into bloody battlegrounds. Journalist and civil rights leader James Weldon Johnson called it a "Red Summer," with violent incidents flaring up in Washington, D.C., Chicago, and Phillips County, Arkansas, as well as in numerous other communities. The violence of the World War I era broke out in East Saint Louis, Illinois, in 1917 and lasted until the worst of the urban race riots erupted at Tulsa, Oklahoma, in 1921.

One cause of the violence was white fear of rural black migrants appearing in the cities. The black mass migration to the cities triggered by the wartime need for factory workers brought about wider social changes. According to the migrants themselves, their chief motivation for leaving the South was to escape the demeaning conditions of segregation. Once in the North, the migrants consolidated older black communities. Many secured factory jobs and improved their standards of living. Those who remained in the South, 80 percent of all African Americans, lived under difficult conditions.

As new black communities in the urban North took shape, established institutions changed to meet the needs of the newcomers. The activities of religious leaders, business owners, social workers, other professionals, and working people aimed at meeting the needs of these expanding black communities. Institutions like the African Methodist Episcopal Church, the Baptist Church, the Urban League, and the African American branches of the Young Men's and Young Women's Christian Association expanded their activities during the 1920s.

Yet, the old problems persisted. Civil rights activists continued the fight against lynching, segregation, disfranchisement, economic oppression, and discrimination in the criminal-justice system. They mobilized against the Ku Klux Klan, which had been established in 1915 and attracted a growing following after World War I. The National Association for the Advancement of Colored People (NAACP) consolidated its all-black leadership in this period and grew rapidly to over three hundred branches with one hundred thousand members by the early 1920s. Although hope for a postwar breakthrough in civil rights soon faltered, civil rights activists worked to improve race relations throughout the decade.

The 1920s also witnessed a public manifestation of emerging pride and national identity among African Americans. The dynamic Marcus Garvey movement emphasized entrepreneurship, solidarity with Africa, and self-help until its sharp decline mid-decade. Black poets, writers, and artists expressed the full range of emotions let loose by black people as they created new communities. Black intellectuals contributed to American life, especially in history and sociology. Musicians found a wide audience among listeners and dancers, and the popularity of jazz and the blues helped to undermine racial hostility. In baseball, thousands of fans attended Negro League games. African American achievement subverted racist myths about black inferiority, made African Americans feel proud of their heritage, and increased their self-confidence. For the first time, black creative artists found an audience among whites and inspired some to learn about African American culture.

Yet, the creative outpouring would fall victim, like so many other things, to the economic depression of the 1930s. The American economy slowed down a few years before the October 1929 stock market crash. Black workers felt the effects first. They had been the last hired and would be the first fired. On the farms, the decline of the price of cotton hit black farmers hardest. Soon, the issue of economic survival thrust all other matters to the bottom of the agenda. Many black institutions, especially businesses, collapsed. But churches, newspapers, and civil rights groups survived. Jazz gained unprecedented popularity during the next world war, and the blues would evolve into rock 'n' roll during the 1950s. The cultural outpouring of the 1920s helped lay the groundwork for the momentous changes that lay ahead for African Americans.

CHAPTER ONE

∿

Black Hopes, White Fears, Red Summer

The end of World War I in November of 1918 unleashed contradictory feelings of hope and frustration, as well as bitterness and pride, among African Americans. Having fought and died for their country abroad, they were resolved to end discrimination at home. As participants in the war in uniform and on the home front, they had gained self-confidence and a sense of solidarity with other black Americans. Yet, their hopes were tempered by realism. Despite some encouraging signs, white America seemed as rooted in its old racist fears as ever. In addition, new economic problems made white racial insecurities more dangerous than before. This volatile mixture of black hopes and white fears produced an unprecedented explosion of racial violence. Civil rights leader and journalist James Weldon Johnson called the outburst the "Red Summer." In six major, and dozens of lesser, confrontations, African Americans confronted white attacks on their communities. The violence began in East St. Louis, Illinois, in 1917, reached a peak in 1919, and continued until the most destructive battle of all in Tulsa, Oklahoma, in 1921. Smaller episodes continued to erupt throughout the decade.

The new mood among black Americans caused them to fight back when whites attacked their communities. The world war had produced a "New Negro." Black journalists used this term to describe the new attitude of their people in the 1920s. New Negroes—veteran or civilian, young or old, female or male—had been transformed by the war. They were proud, not easily intimidated, and determined to win their rights.

The veterans played an important part in creating the new mood. They showed that black men had courage, a fact that most white people denied.

Almost four hundred thousand black soldiers served, half of them in France, and thirty thousand of these had seen battle. Of the four black combat regiments, the best known was the New York 369th Colored Infantry. Dubbed "Hellfighters" by their French allies and "Bloodthirsty Black Men" by the German enemy, the former National Guard regiment fought in the trenches for 191 days. Their most famous hero, Sergeant Henry Johnson, killed or captured over twenty Germans. One lesson of the war was that black soldiers could face and kill a white enemy. Black soldiers also learned that not all white people were hostile. The French knew that the black soldiers were fighting for them, and they showed their gratitude spontaneously, by shaking hands with the men or sharing their food. The French loved the 369th's regimental band, led by Lieutenant James Reese Europe, and thronged to hear its jazzy melodies and expressive horn sounds.

But African Americans learned their most important lesson of the war from each other. Before the war, few black people had traveled at all, and they had little sense of their own combined numbers and strength. Now men from Cleveland and Washington, D.C., mixed with soldiers from rural Georgia and Texas. In trenches or at Young Men's Christian Association (YMCA) huts, they talked among themselves, shared the experience of war, and compared their situations at home. Here they were, fighting for someone else's freedom abroad, while they had none in America. This contradiction was troubling.

Moreover, black soldiers were acutely aware of discrimination in the army. Draft boards were lily white and refused to consider legitimate claims that black people had for exemption from duty. Black officers trained at a segregated facility in Des Moines, Iowa, and were treated with contempt by white officers. African Americans could only fight in combat under French command because the American generals disdained them. Black combat units were undersupplied and poorly instructed in the use of arms. Stevedores were often poorly clothed, handling cold steel armaments without gloves in the chill of winter. And there were plenty of fights with white soldiers, who were unnerved by the sight of black men at war. On the home front, government agents harassed black dissidents and threatened antiwar newspapers. Black soldiers returned home not only with a sense of a mission accomplished but with resentment at these indignities.

The fateful year of 1919 began on a note of hope for improved race relations. On February 17, twenty-nine hundred black soldiers marched north through Manhattan up to Harlem. Thousands of New Yorkers, black and white, lined the parade route and cheered. James Reese Europe led his regimental band, and Sergeant Henry Johnson greeted the crowd from an open car, his Croix de Guerre gleaming on his uniform. Dignitaries and white elected officials waved from a reviewing stand. Such a day would have been unimaginable before the war.

Still, amid the celebration, the struggle continued. Two days after the New York parade, William Edward Burghardt DuBois, editor of the National Association for the Advancement of Colored People's (NAACP) *Crisis* magazine and the most prominent African American intellectual in the country, opened a Pan-African Congress in Paris. Delegates from sixteen nations of Africa and its diaspora considered resolutions that demanded increased political autonomy and better economic conditions in the colonies. Few whites paid attention, but the congress represented a first step toward the independence of African nations that would come after World War II.

Three months later, the NAACP convened a dramatic antilynching conference in New York City. Under the direction of association president Moorfield Storey, distinguished speakers, including Supreme Court Justice Charles Evans Hughes, Attorney General A. Mitchell Palmer, former Alabama governor Emmett O'Neal, and suffragist Anna Howard Shaw addressed an interracial audience at Carnegie Hall. They argued that lynching was a horrible crime whose purpose was to suppress all black people, that it subverted the rule of law, and that it shamed America before the world. But what could be done about it? The conference was not yet ready to insist upon a federal antilynching law. Within a few years, the NAACP would take this step, but in 1919, even civil rights advocates thought it would have little chance of passing. At the least, the organizers hoped to sway public opinion following black participation in the war. Other black groups, including the National Equal Rights League, the National Race Congress, and the National Baptist Convention, also protested lynching. Black newspapers covered these meetings enthusiastically, but white dailies scarcely noticed them.

Another sign of the new mood was the spurt in growth of the NAACP and its change to black central leadership. At its national convention in Cleveland, Ohio, thousands of activists arrived determined to build the movement. A few months later, lawmen from Austin, Texas, on a busy street, severely beat John Shillady, the white secretary of the NAACP, for asserting the NAACP's right to exist. No Texas lawyer had the courage to sue the city. Discouraged, Shillady resigned his post, and James Weldon Johnson became the first black national secretary of the civil rights group.

While African Americans strengthened their organizations, white Americans became more fearful about the shaky economic outlook and blamed black people for their troubles. At the end of World War I, the economy went into crisis. Munitions factories shut down just as hundreds of thousands of men demobilized and sought jobs. Industrial bosses, chafing under the authority of wartime government boards that encouraged them to pay decent wages so as to avoid labor strife, vowed to drive wages down. They forced strikes in a number of key industries, especially in meat packing, steel production, and coal mining. In place of the strikers they hired black replacement workers, who desperately needed the money. The black workers had no love for the whites, who had banned them from their unions for decades. This economic tension caused much racial violence in 1919.

In addition, an earlier public health disaster, which did not distinguish between whites and blacks, contributed to the atmosphere of anxiety. In 1918 an influenza epidemic killed millions around the world and hundreds of thousands of Americans. Because urban black people lived closely crowded together, a disproportionate number of them died of this virus. In dozens of cities, bodies piled up in morgues for weeks until the epidemic mercifully stopped as mysteriously as it began. The survivors became increasingly fearful.

African Americans demanding civil rights did so in a climate dominated by suspicion of dissent. Before the war, Americans showed hostility to German and Irish Americans who opposed U.S. participation. Afterward, in 1919, anarchists, many of whom were Italian immigrants, initiated a wave of bombings, hoping to destabilize capitalist society. One bomber blew himself up on the doorstep of Attorney General A. Mitchell Palmer's home. Communists staged noisy parades on May Day and organized a political party. The radicals generated a backlash against those who asserted their identities as anything but fully "American." Government repression of the radicals culminated in a wave of mass arrests and threatened deportations of immigrants in January 1920. The civil rights movement therefore had to stress its "American" character and to downplay the idea that it was fighting for African American rights.

The general chaos in American society took attention away from race relations, further undermining African American hopes for civil rights. The burning issue of the day was President Woodrow Wilson's effort to get Congress to accept the peace treaty that he had helped negotiate with the European allies. But Congress balked at his inclusion of a League of Nations in the treaty. Wilson set off on a national speaking tour and suffered a serious stroke, which left him incapacitated, and the nation leaderless as the president's wife and doctor covered up his illness. Of more direct interest to millions, the country had amended the Constitution to ban the sale of liquor. People who wanted a drink would have to break the law to have one. Even the World Series did not go as expected. Gamblers had paid the White Sox to lose, a symptom of the labor troubles of the day. African Americans clearly had nothing to do with these matters, but all these problems distracted the public from addressing the civil rights concerns of black people.

The one social change that favored African American aspirations was that women won the right to vote in 1920. The suffrage amendment broadened the notion of inclusion in the body politic. It suggested that all citizens should have unrestricted access to the ballot, and black women in the South would try to take advantage of it in the 1920 election.

Taken as a whole, the rapid changes and conflicts of the year after the war led many white people to look for a scapegoat for their troubles. Capitalists caused the strikes, a virus caused the flu, and stubborn politicians caused the diplomatic chaos. Yet, during the Red Summer, white Americans blamed a familiar victim. They soon learned, however, that the New Negro would no longer serve as anybody's scapegoat.

African Americans showed this new attitude in Charleston, South Carolina, after white sailors killed a black civilian on May 10, 1919. Fighting broke out between the two groups, and the mayor asked the Marines to help police quell the violence. When it was over, two black citizens were dead and seventeen were wounded, and eight white sailors were wounded. The city perceived the white sailors as outsiders and troublemakers. The navy wanted good relations with the host city and established an investigative board. Prompted by the NAACP, it found six white sailors guilty of serious charges, including manslaughter. Black property owners unsuccessfully pressed the city to compensate them for damages. The Charleston riot showed that the New Negroes would fight white attacks with defensive violence, political pressure, and legal proceedings.

African Americans organized armed self-defense two months later in Longview, Texas. The trouble began when the bullet-filled corpse of Lemuel Walters, a black man, was discovered outside of town. It turned out that Walters had had a white lover. When leaders of the black community demanded that the killer be brought to justice, the authorities told them to keep quiet. An anonymous letter, published in the nationally circulated *Chicago Defender*, protested the murder and cover-up. Whites accused S. L. Jones, a black Longview high school teacher, of being the author. They assaulted him on the street and told him to get out of town. A mob attacked his home at night, but African Americans fought them off, shooting four whites. This was a clear sign of the new mood among African Americans. The next day whites attacked the black community, torching homes at random until the militia restored order. About twenty whites and twenty blacks were arrested, and by the end of the month, Longwood had quieted down.

Meanwhile, in the nation's capital, racial conflict was heating up. In late July, the *Washington Post* reported a series of alleged attacks on white women by a black assailant. The false story led to confrontations between blacks and whites in the streets. The *Post* printed a craftily worded appeal for off-duty white servicemen to assemble on Pennsylvania Avenue, which led to the formation of a bloodthirsty mob. The hoodlums attacked the black community for five days, and the military had to be called up to quell the violence. Blacks and whites battled with guns, leaving killed and wounded on both sides. NAACP leader James Weldon Johnson visited the city during the riot, praised black people for defending themselves, and castigated the newspaper for its irresponsibility. It later turned out that the *Post* had been feuding with the city commissioner on an unrelated matter and wanted to discredit him as an incompetent administrator by provoking the riot.

The worst urban rioting of 1919 broke out in Chicago during the last five days of July. An African American swimmer, who had drifted into waters between segregated beaches, drowned when a white man threw a rock and hit him. The youth's companions found a black policeman, but white officers obstructed the arrest of the assailant. Rumors began to fly, and in the summer heat, emotions boiled over into violence. Chief among the perpetrators were Irish youth gangs. After the beach incident, the gangs began assaulting black people at random. The police stationed men along the neighborhood's racial divide, Wentworth Avenue, but this tactic left scant protection for black workers entering white areas to get to their jobs. The next day, white hooligans killed several black men as they left their jobs in the stockyards. A few white men who later crossed into the black community at 35th and State streets met the same fate. Whites retaliated by driving through the black community, spraying gunfire. Undeterred, a crowd of black men gathered at an apartment house on Wabash Avenue, where a white sniper was hiding. Police arrived at the scene, somebody threw a stone, and the police opened fire, killing four African Americans in the crowd. White mobs stormed the black community, and roving stick, knife, and gun fights broke out. Some policemen joined the white marauders, and many looked the other way when whites were getting the best of a fight.

Unlike Charleston and Washington officials, Chicago authorities refused to call out the National Guard. This failure prolonged the rioting. A transit strike exacerbated a bad situation by raising the number of black people who had to walk through hostile white neighborhoods. White newspapers fanned the violence by reporting unsubstantiated atrocity stories. The violence did not subside until the militia was called up in force, and rain drove people indoors. It took another week for twelve thousand African American stock-yard workers to return to work under heavy police guard. Thousands of white workers threatened to walk out in protest. After two weeks of trouble, officials counted 23 blacks and 15 whites dead, and 342 blacks and 195 whites injured.

The Chicago riot was deeply rooted in the social tensions brought about by the Great Migration. In effect, white thugs vented their frustrations about postwar life on new black migrants. Chicago African Americans were securing jobs, expanding their community geographically, developing political power, and demanding police protection and justice in the courts. Many white residents were determined to keep the newcomers in second-class citizenship status in all of these areas.

The most important cause of the Chicago riot was white working-class hostility to black workers. Black workers had been hired as strikebreakers in Chicago's packinghouse industry as early as 1894, and there had been other incidents of strikebreaking over the years. White workers had kept black men out of their unions, and the new arrivals knew that taking these jobs was their only hope. In 1919, Chicago, with two hundred fifty thousand strikers, was the focal point of the national labor turmoil. White union leaders in the meatpacking industry, having learned from past experience, tried to recruit black workers, but their efforts were too little and came too late. They could not overcome the hostility of rank-and-file whites, who believed that black workers were fit only for the worst jobs. African American community leaders—ministers, newspaper editors, and social service agency heads—differed in their attitude toward unions. Some wished for improved relations with them, but others thought that black-labor solidarity was a hopeless cause and that chances for advancement lay only in cooperation with employers.

The housing shortage also contributed to racial tension. A small number of middle-class African Americans could afford houses in all-white neighborhoods. A few working-class blacks also integrated Hyde Park, a "white" neighborhood that bordered the Black Belt. Racist realtors and homeowners figured that this process would drive down the value of their property. They formed associations whose explicit purpose was to prevent black people from buying homes in "their" neighborhoods. They put clauses in the deeds that forbade sales to black buyers and, when that failed, they turned to violence. Between 1917 and 1919, twenty-six bombs exploded at black homes, one of which killed a young girl. The police proved curiously incapable of finding the terrorists. The *Chicago Defender* and the *Whip*, leading black community newspapers, urged vigilant self-defense.

In addition, black Chicago's growing political strength further antagonized working-class whites. Black voters provided Republican mayor William "Big Bill" Thompson with his margin of victory in two mayoral elections, including a tight race in 1919. The city's Irish American Democrats especially hated Thompson, whom they accused of being anti-Catholic. They blamed black voters for their enemy's victory. Thompson had also alienated the state's governor, who headed a rival Republican faction. That explained why Thompson was reluctant to call out the state militia during the riot.

Finally, the conduct of the Chicago police department and the state of mind of the New Negro made the simmering racial tensions especially explosive. The police department was thoroughly prejudiced, and the worst of its members either assisted the white rioters or ignored assaults on African Americans. Young black men, especially those who had just returned from the war, were in no mood to respond meekly to insult. Police indifference to the killing of a black youth, the cause of the riot, was no longer something Chicago African Americans were willing to tolerate as a normal state of affairs.

A different pattern of racial violence surfaced next in Knoxville, Tennessee. In August 1919, a mob determined to lynch prisoner Maurice Mays, an African American, stormed the jail. White mobs felt entitled to take the law into their own hands, especially when a black man was accused of molesting a white woman. The authorities usually made some show of resisting the mobs, but not at the cost of taking white life. This ambivalent approach never worked in the extreme emergencies that lynch mobs presented.

On August 30, Knoxville police arrested Mays and accused him of murdering a white woman. The police quickly moved Mays to Chattanooga for protection, but a mob sacked the jail and turned all of the white prisoners loose. City authorities called out the National Guard to prevent the mob from burning the African American district, but in the process, the guard killed two black residents. Fifty whites were arrested for their participation in the violence, but almost all were acquitted. There is strong evidence that Mays was innocent, as similar attacks on women continued after his arrest. Moreover, survivors of later attacks identified a swarthy white assailant, and Mays was a light-skinned black man. In addition, he was active in an anti–Ku

Klux Klan political faction, and the police force was riddled with Klansmen. Despite a vigorous defense effort, Mays was convicted and executed.

A similar scenario developed at the end of September in Omaha, Nebraska. There the police failed to prevent the lynching of their prisoner, whose guilt was also doubtful. The mayor confronted the white mob personally but was unwilling to use force to disperse it. The crowd seized the mayor and was about to hang him before the police came to his aid. Then, the mob broke into the jail, murdered the accused prisoner, set fire to his corpse, and posed for a celebratory picture around the charred body. Too late for the victim, federal troops marched into town and placed it under martial law. As in Knoxville, whites were arrested, and some went to trial. In both cities, many of the rioters were common criminals acting on their own antipolice agenda.

In early February 1920, state authorities broke the familiar pattern. In Lexington, Kentucky, Republican governor Edwin P. Morrow ordered the National Guard commander to protect the prisoner at all costs. In perhaps the only case in American history, guardsmen fired into a lynch mob outside a courthouse where a black man was about to go on trial. About four thousand frightened white men ran away. Six were killed and fifty wounded. Had this pattern been established earlier and repeated a few times, perhaps future lynch mob participants would have calculated the risks involved. The story made banner headlines in the African American press but appeared mostly on the back pages in white dailies. The NAACP cabled Governor Morrow its congratulations. Few people noticed, but the accused man, who was mentally retarded and had confessed to killing a white girl, was found guilty.

A more typical tragedy unfolded in Duluth, Minnesota, in June, where three black circus hands were accused of raping a white woman. The likelihood in this case is that the alleged victim and her lover invented the crime. Still, a large crowd burst past the token resistance put up by police. The mob seized the young men, Elmer Jackson, Ellis Clayton, and Isaac McGhee, beat them, and hung them one at a time from lampposts. Middle-class Duluth was profoundly shocked, and Minnesota's governor was embarrassed. The NAACP demanded prosecution of the instigators, and its Minneapolis, St. Paul, and Duluth branches sprang into action. Twelve white men were arrested and charged with murder, and another eighteen were indicted on lesser charges. Apparently, however, no one was convicted. A grand jury report blamed Duluth's law-enforcement leaders on the scene, and the chief of police was forced to resign. His reason for failing to quell the lynch mob was that shooting might have injured innocent women and children. This logic, common in the 1920s, led to the deaths of many black prisoners not yet brought to trial. In 2003, Duluth unveiled a memorial to the victims. It is perhaps the only such public monument that acknowledges the plague of lynching in the United States.

Another familiar pattern of racial violence was terrorism designed to prevent black people from voting. This had been the purpose of the original Ku Klux Klan during the Reconstruction era after the Civil War, and it continued in the Klan that formed again in 1915. On Election Day in 1920, an armed confrontation at the polls led to the destruction of the black community at Ocoee, Florida, near Orlando. White vigilantes prevented several black people from voting and pursued them to the African American district. Jules Perry, a black man, shot two intruders dead when they threatened his home. In response, whites burned the whole community to the ground, killing at least six people, including a mother and child. The terrified inhabitants fled into the woods. The white-owned press downplayed the incident, and because Ocoee was relatively isolated, the black press did not get the story until much later, when a survivor of the massacre gave her account of the events.

An event unique among postwar racial conflicts occurred in Phillips County, Arkansas, a heavily African American region along the Mississippi River in cotton country. Black tenant farmers there had banded together to insist on a fair price for their crops. Consumer goods were scarce, and white landlords anticipated that they would be able cheat their tenants by lying about cotton's rising market value. They infiltrated the tenants' group by hiring a black detective. For reasons that remain unclear, a nighttime gunfight began outside a meeting of African Americans that left one white man dead and another wounded. The next day, white vigilantes on both sides of the Mississippi mobilized by the thousands and began shooting blacks on sight. At least twenty-five were killed, and one black leader claimed that the death toll might have been as high as two hundred. Five whites died, although it is likely that these were killed by friendly fire.

The speed and viciousness of the white mobilization and the scattered nature of the resistance suggests that the landlords had decided to break the union by a surprise military strike. The governor finally called out federal troops, who rounded up hundreds of black farmers and held them at Helena, the county seat. These men were interrogated and, if spoken for by their landlord, generally released. Many, especially black farmers who owned their land, were not so lucky. A grand jury indicted 122 black men, charging 73 with murder.

Two groups of six prisoners each were swiftly convicted of murder and sentenced to death. Another sixty-seven were convicted of lesser charges and sentenced to twenty years in prison. The trials were conducted hastily as a crowd of angry whites menaced the court building, and the "defense" lawyers openly sided with the prosecution. A committee of white farmers working with county officials extracted incriminating evidence from other prisoners by torturing them. The juries reached their verdicts in under an hour. The death sentences were to be carried out within a few weeks. One of the worst massacres in American history was thus followed by one of the worst judicial proceedings since the Salem witch trials.

White Arkansas newspapers concluded that the verdicts were satisfactory. They reported the fantastic story that the defendants had conspired to kill leading whites in the county and stage an ill-defined revolution. An aide to the governor explained in a confidential letter that by acting firmly, the authorities had suppressed a black uprising. Newspapers around the country covered these events on their front pages, but no newspaper sent a reporter to the scene. There was a bigger story that month—the strange defeat of the Chicago White Sox in the World Series.

Faced with such blatant discrimination, blacks fought back through legal means. Black leaders at Little Rock, Arkansas, organized a defense committee to appeal the verdicts and organized a campaign to lobby the governor. Moreover, they contacted the national NAACP, although they worried that outside public pressure would cause the white power structure to close ranks. This was a constant dilemma for Southern civil rights activists. Even "liberal" Southern whites, those who wanted fair treatment of black people within the segregationist framework, instinctively became protective of their state's reputation when "outsiders" criticized the most blatant atrocities. Most important, no white politician could yield to pressure from black people and expect to be reelected. The Little Rock black leaders understood this dilemma and tried to protect the imprisoned men without publicly accusing state authorities.

National civil rights leaders were in a different situation. They did not have to live with the hostility that would be created locally by directly confronting the authorities. Their goal was to ensure enforcement of the Fourteenth Amendment, which guaranteed national protection of individual citizens' rights. An inevitable tension developed between national civil rights leaders and the more cautious local black leaders. Ida B. Wells-Barnett, the venerable antilynching campaigner, and Walter White of the NAACP, made separate trips to Arkansas to report on what had happened. Throughout the defense effort, national leaders and local activists sparred over tactics and financial issues.

Regardless of their differences with the national NAACP, local black leaders raised money and helped organize the defense in Arkansas. Scipio Africanus Jones, a black attorney and community activist, argued the appeals over the next five years. Sometimes assisted by white attorneys whose presence in court lent more legitimacy to his pleading, Jones appeared in every possible Arkansas venue to plead for the condemned men. The cases were separated into two groups of six, and each proceeded through different courts, raising different issues, in different parts of the state. He argued that no evidence showed that any of the defendants had killed anyone. Moreover, the authorities prosecuted no whites despite the deaths of dozens, if not hundreds, of black people. Most importantly for an appeals process, there had not been a shred of legality in the original trials. Arkansas justice had mocked the right of a citizen to a fair trial.

The NAACP took the case, known as *Moore v. Dempsey*, to the U.S. Supreme Court in 1924. Its president and leading attorney, Moorfield Storey, followed the argument that Scipio Jones had advanced. He stipulated that the accused men had not had a fair trial, and therefore their Fourteenth Amendment rights had been violated. Storey showed that the Arkansas trials were fraudulent and invalid by national standards. Justice Oliver Wendell Holmes wrote the majority opinion, invalidating the Arkansas decisions. Rather than retry the cases, Arkansas authorities decided to commute the death sentences and quietly furloughed the prisoners. In this fashion, white Arkansas saved face, and the men went free with no publicity. Scipio Jones, his Arkansas colleagues, and the national civil rights community had won a signal legal victory.

Moore v. Dempsey helped expand the meaning of the Fourteenth Amendment, whose original intent was to assure equality before the law. In the years after its 1868 passage, the Supreme Court had consistently ruled to constrict its interpretation so as to render it meaningless. Southern prosecutors barred African Americans from juries, framed them on the flimsiest of evidence, denied them meaningful representation, and permitted prejudicial atmospheres inside courtrooms. The *Moore* decision represented the first sign by the Supreme Court that there were limits to what states could do.

The final major race riot of the period tore through Tulsa, Oklahoma, for twenty-four violent hours beginning on the night of May 31, 1921. The violence began after a white female elevator operator claimed that a black youth, who had stumbled against her due to the elevator's motion, had "assaulted" her. The young man was arrested and jailed. Angry whites gathered outside. Fanning the flames of popular racism, a local newspaper headline blared, "To Lynch Negro Tonight." Armed black men, many of them World War I veterans, went to the jail to prevent the lynching. With the memory of a previous lynching fresh in their minds, they were determined to prevent another one. The black Tulsans felt reassured when they found the police adequately prepared to defend the prisoner, who could only be approached by a narrow, heavily guarded staircase. But as the black crowd dispersed, a white man tried to disarm a black man, and shooting started.

In 1921, eleven thousand African Americans lived in Tulsa, most of them in the Greenwood neighborhood, which was remarkably prosperous. Indeed, it was known as the Black Wall Street. Tulsa's economy boomed with oil profits, and black workers found employment in a variety of businesses. The city was segregated, and the demand for services by working-class black people produced an enterprising middle class of store owners and professionals. The black community boasted two newspapers, schools, a hospital, thirteen churches, theaters, and a library.

Historians have not yet determined how many African Americans were killed in Tulsa. There are higher and lower estimates, but the middle figure is about seventy-five. Hundreds of others were injured. The rampaging vandals looted and burned the whole district, stealing property before setting fire to homes. Churches, stores, lodge buildings, and theaters were put to the torch. Over one thousand homes were destroyed, and hundreds of others looted. Thousands of black people fled the city, while the National Guard rounded up thousands of others and interned them in makeshift camps.

When the violence was over, many black Tulsans had to spend the winter living in tents. African American organizations contributed emergency relief funds, but the city of Tulsa did little. Tulsa even tried to pass an ordinance requiring stricter building codes, hoping it would inhibit the rebuilding efforts of black residents. Almost fourteen hundred black Tulsans sued to reclaim $4 million in property damages. Despite the obstacles, the Greenwood district rose from the ashes and served as an inspiration to black people throughout the country.

A notable aspect of the Tulsa riot was that white casualties were high. Tulsa was a typical Western city and many men, including African Americans, owned guns. The Oklahoma City *Black Dispatch* probably exaggerated when it reported that whites and blacks died in equal numbers, but it is true that white riots of this type dramatically declined after the Tulsa incident. This was probably due mostly to the prosperity of the 1920s, but the determined resistance of black Tulsans may have convinced violent whites that there was a price to pay for racial mayhem.

Black resistance at Tulsa did not end the plague of violence against African Americans during the 1920s, but it helped diminish it. Smaller incidents continued, and two of them highlighted the gender dimension of racial tensions. At Rosewood, Florida, and Coffeyville, Kansas, quarreling white lovers invented black assaults on the women, similar to the triggering incident in Duluth. The couples' motivations were not always clear in these cases, but they typically combined ignorance about reproduction, the need to cover something up, and hostility to black men.

In Rosewood, on New Year's Day 1923, a white married woman living in the nearby town of Sumner, fought with her lover inside her home. To explain her bruises to her husband, she claimed that a black intruder had assaulted her. She probably knew that a black prisoner had recently escaped from a chain gang and would be a likely suspect. Vigilantes accused two men in the nearby all-black town of Rosewood of aiding the escapee and alleged rapist. After torturing one of them to get a confession, a mob returned a few days later. They shot down a black woman in her doorway, and a protracted gunfight broke out, leaving two whites dead. The white invaders retreated and regrouped. Meanwhile, Rosewood's women and children fled into the woods at night and were exposed to the elements. A handful of sympathetic whites helped them escape, but the attackers returned and overwhelmed the town's defenders, killing several. Then, they sacked the town, killing even the farm animals and burning it to the ground. Not one white person was prosecuted, and the story was scarcely reported except in the African American press.

The aftermath of this tragedy suggests that the country may be beginning to come to terms with the horrors of the past. Seventy years later, the granddaughter of the white woman's maid came forward to describe what she had seen. She had been in the house and seen the white lover. The Florida newspapers reported her testimony, and the descendants of the townspeople came forward to ask for reparations. The state legislature approved a cash compensation for each survivor and established a scholarship fund for the descendants. Black filmmaker John Singleton's 1997 movie *Rosewood* helped make this once obscure event one of the era's better-known incidents.

In 1927, a similar incident in Coffeyville, Kansas, produced a startlingly different outcome from the Rosewood massacre. Two white girls, after an evening of cavorting with some boys, claimed afterward that three black men had raped them. Although they could provide no description of the alleged assailants, the police rounded up three bewildered suspects. Sure enough, a lynch mob showed up at the prison, but this time lawmen drove the mob off. The throng headed for the black community, and a gunfight resulted in injuries on both sides. When the relationship between the two girls deteriorated, the younger one told the truth. The Coffeyville authorities then did an unusual thing: they dropped all charges against the accused men, and prosecuted a white man and the older girl. They were acquitted, but most white officials in the 1920s would not have admitted their mistake as did the Coffeyville people. By 1927, perhaps, times had changed enough to make this outcome possible, outside the South at least.

The postwar racial violence had several longer-term effects. It deepened the rift between the races and caused bitterness and alienation among African Americans. It also showed the country that black people were determined to fight back when attacked. For New Negroes, their own response emboldened them to feel that they could rely upon each other, and it made their emerging communities stronger.

Of course, there was more taking place than just violence. The Red Summer unfolded in the context of a Great Migration northward. Chapter 2 discusses how the migration changed African America and the United States as a whole.

CHAPTER TWO

~

Migrants North

During the 1920s, African Americans voted against Jim Crow with their feet. They left the South in greater numbers than ever before so that, by the end of the decade, about one-fifth of the nation's nearly twelve million African Americans lived in the North. Their movement said to all who cared to notice that black people were fed up with discrimination. The migration set the stage for an even larger population shift after World War II.

The movement north led to greater economic gains for African Americans, providing the only chance for advancement. Rural people became urbanites, many of them industrial workers. Nonetheless, in 1930 almost 80 percent of African Americans still lived in the rural South, most of them eking out a hard existence as sharecroppers.

Many factors caused the migration, but the most important was disgust with the Jim Crow system. In letters to Northern relatives, the migrants made clear what was uppermost in their minds. Black people had to defer to whites in every interaction with them. They had to endure segregation in all public places from streetcars to the post office. In stores, they could not try on clothing. In movie theaters, they sat in a separate section in the balcony. Daily life was characterized by constant humiliation.

In addition, any showing of resentment against this state of affairs could provoke white violence. An individual could be beaten or killed just for talking back to an insulting white person. Racial violence shamed and angered black people, who could do very little to prevent it. Letters to the Chicago *Defender* provide numerous examples of African Americans who left the South because of this situation.

Another factor pushing people out of the South was the failure of the cotton crop during those years. In 1915, a plague of boll weevils destroyed the plants and left thousands of farmers destitute. In the mid-1920s, when harvests improved, the price of cotton dropped steeply, causing more farm failures. In South Carolina especially, African American farmers were squeezed by these economic problems and departed in droves.

Black women may have had their own special reasons for leaving. Some were running away from violent or predatory men, both white and black. Black women in the South rarely reported rape to the police, who did not bother to investigate the complaints of black crime victims. Other women left violent fathers who were beating them or their mothers, and some abandoned their abusive husbands. Despite the fact that travel by single women had its own hazards, many took their chances, usually heading for the home of a Northern relative.

Women especially became links in the migration chain because of their role as nurturers within the family. Some had to leave children behind at least temporarily, until they were secure enough in their new lives. The children might stay with a near relative until their mothers could bring them to the new home. On the return trip, they might boast of their new favorable conditions and convince a cousin or sibling to join them on the journey back.

A corresponding set of attractions pulled black people to the North. While the newly expanded Northern black communities offered their share of hardships, they often felt exhilaratingly free to people accustomed to segregation. The author Richard Wright, who migrated to Chicago from Mississippi, was astonished to find that he could sit next to white people on the streetcar, and they seemed to pay it no mind. The writer Rudolph Fisher penned a short story, "City of Refuge," in which a rural migrant to Manhattan was amazed to see a black policeman. In Northern cities, African Americans could report a crime to the police, serve on juries, orate on street corners, and vote. If these rights were violated, they might at least appeal to the courts. Northern cities offered better schooling and social services, which were scarcely available in the rural South. Whatever problems life in the North entailed, most migrants improved their situation by moving there.

Furthermore, African Americans came north to get good jobs. They learned about economic opportunities through relatives already living there, through "race" papers like the Chicago *Defender* that circulated in the South, and occasionally through labor recruiters who sought employees for a particular industry. Typically, a young man would leave for the North first and later send money for rail fare to relatives who had remained in the South. Migrants sometimes had to plan their escape carefully from grasping landlords who warned railroad ticket agents not to allow "their Negroes" to leave.

Although the economy was in recession from 1919 to 1921, and Northern white workers were often hostile to them, most migrants improved their financial situations. Many became industrial workers in the expanding auto industry of Detroit, the steel mills of Pittsburgh, the stockyards of Chicago, the coal mines of West Virginia, or the diverse manufacturing centers of New York, Philadelphia, and Cleveland. Black workers in Pittsburgh could earn over $2 a day, more than double the average wage in the South. In Chicago, the wage might be as high as forty-eight cents an hour. Meanwhile, a Georgia cotton picker could earn about fifty cents for a day's toil under the hot sun. A maid might earn $8 a week plus room and board in the North, but less than half of that in the South. For many black people, migration meant jobs and freedom.

One sign of the improvement in the quality of African American life during the 1920s was a rise in black birth rates and a decline in death rates. Although blacks still declined as a percentage of the total population between 1920 and 1930, the rate of decline was slowing. Meanwhile a change in immigration laws meant that white population growth was also slowing and that African Americans would play a more significant role in the labor force in the future.

Still, the biggest change in the national demographic picture was the migration, causing the U.S. Department of the Census to issue a lengthy special report in 1935. It demonstrated that the migration was the most significant demographic shift in the black population in all of African American history. For 120 years, 90 percent of African Americans had lived in the South. Between 1910 and 1920, that figure had dropped nearly 5 percent, and by 1930 it had dropped an additional 6.5 percent. The phenomenon of the Great Migration continued throughout the decade.

Several states showed dramatic gains in African American population during the 1920s. Michigan's black population increased at the fastest rate, gaining 169,000 people. The African American populations of California, New York, and Wisconsin more than doubled. Illinois, New Jersey, and Ohio had the fifth, sixth, and seventh largest black populations of all states, with a combined 360,000 black residents. Pennsylvania, Nebraska, and Connecticut rounded out the top ten states in percentage growth. In absolute numbers, New York showed the biggest population gain of 214,331 people; Pennsylvania had the largest Northern black population with 431,257 people. Meanwhile, most Southern states lost black residents. Almost a quarter of a million black people left Georgia, South Carolina, and Virginia alone.

African Americans were not just moving north, they were also moving to cities in the South. In 1920, over 3.5 million African Americans lived in urban areas; by 1930, the figure rose to 5.2 million, or 43.7 percent of the black population. The majority of them lived in cities with more than twenty-five thousand people.

The migrants came especially to the big cities. New York's black population soared from 152,467 in 1920 to 327,706 a decade later. Manhattan's Harlem district became the capital of black America, attracting migrants from all over the South and immigrants from the West Indies. Chicago's black community also more than doubled in size to 233,903, making it the second largest black community, with Philadelphia following closely behind. Population sizes dropped off sharply after that in the next seven largest cities: Baltimore, Washington, D.C., New Orleans, Detroit, Birmingham, Memphis, and St. Louis.

These new migrants generally clustered together in one part of the city, forming a visible black community. Prior to the migration, black people frequently lived among European immigrants in mixed neighborhoods. Given the pervasive racism of American society, many African Americans preferred to avoid the meddling and derision of whites. The case of New York City's five boroughs provides a model for what happened in many American cities. Pockets of black settlement existed in several Manhattan neighborhoods before 1915: the Five Points in downtown, the Tenderloin and San Juan Hill on the West Side. Then, the extension of the subway line uptown made it possible to commute to work from much farther away. The uptown Harlem district, constructed on handsome broad avenues and featuring beautiful new apartments, evolved into a middle-class black community. Churches from around the city relocated uptown, bringing their parishioners with them. Gradually, blacks from all social classes moved into Harlem from the other neighborhoods, forming a central and unified black community as whites moved out. By 1930, almost 225,000 of the city's black residents lived in Manhattan, mostly in Harlem. By contrast, fewer than twenty thousand lived on Staten Island, in the Bronx, or in Queens. Brooklyn maintained a distinct black community of almost seventy thousand residents, mostly living in one neighborhood.

A similar pattern unfolded in Chicago, although that city had been more segregated than New York before the migration. The South Side was already home to 78 percent of black Chicagoans by 1910. This was a narrow north-south strip with South Street at its center, extending for over thirty blocks. By 1930, about two-thirds of Chicago's black residents lived in neighborhoods that were over 90 percent black. After the race riot of 1919, many African Americans probably decided it was safest to stay away from white people, who had proved themselves to be unpredictably violent. Thus, in the 1920s, the Northern black experience became mostly segregated.

The process of "ghetto formation," or "black community emergence," was slower in most other Northern cities. Detroit's black community had the fastest rate of growth in the 1920s, but its people were more spread out than those of New York or Chicago. Only a few neighborhoods were more than half African American by 1930, and one-third of all black Detroiters lived in districts that were 10 to 20 percent black. Roughly the same kind of population distribution appeared in Philadelphia, Baltimore, Washington, D.C., Birmingham, and New Orleans. One factor that contributed to this residential pattern in border and Southern cities was probably that many black women worked as maids and had to walk to work. Thus, there was no real equivalent to the Harlem district in Atlanta, whose black residents made up a much greater percentage (one-third) of the total population, but who lived over a more widely dispersed geographic area.

Rural African American Southerners also moved to cities in the South. Houston's black population almost doubled in size during the 1920s. The Memphis black community increased dramatically to number 96,550 people. Baltimore, the fourth largest city in black America, reached 142,106 black residents by 1930, a population growth of 31.2 percent. The next largest Southern black populations lived in Washington, D.C., New Orleans, Birmingham, Memphis, St. Louis, and Atlanta.

In Southern cities, black migrants could more easily maintain ties with their rural relatives. A column in the Norfolk, Virginia, black community newspaper reported frequent visits from relatives, mostly women renewing ties with close family members. Thus, migration did not necessarily represent a total break with one's past; nor was it always a plunge from the close-knit village to an isolating, anonymous big city.

African Americans migrated west as well as north. The West offered the advantages of the North, as well as a more familiar climate. Several Western cities had diverse populations including Mexicans, Chinese, and Native Americans. Los Angeles became the most significant Western black city during the Jazz Age. Its population more than doubled, reaching 38,894 by 1930. By 1918, it had elected the first black state assemblyman in California. Black Angelenos worked at hard jobs in factories and on the docks, but they could also land jobs as extras in Hollywood movies. Black workers purchased goods and services along Central Avenue from burgeoning black-owned businesses. These included a movie theater, banks, an insurance company, and an auto dealership, as well as grocery and clothing stores. The jewel in the crown was the Hotel Somerville, which hosted the 1928 National Association for the Advancement of Colored People (NAACP) convention. W. E. B. DuBois wrote rapturously about black Los Angeles.

Black San Antonio grew very little during the 1920s but it adapted well to its opportunities. It sits at the gateway to heavily Mexican American South and West Texas. During the 1920s, African Americans collaborated with Mexican Americans to deliver their votes to one Democratic Party faction. In return, they got a better share of city services. African Americans in the West found Native Americans in Oklahoma, Chinese Americans in San Francisco, and Japanese Americans in California's Central Valley or Seattle to be fellow outcasts from white society. They sometimes ignored each other, sometimes made common cause, and sometimes competed as small-business owners.

Another change in the makeup of the black population was the migration of black West Indians to the United States. The immigration restriction laws of the 1920s did not limit these immigrants because they were counted under the quotas for the European countries that ruled them. By 1930, about fifty-four thousand West Indians lived in New York. Miami and Boston also had small West Indian communities. While many Americans regarded these migrants as one undifferentiated group, they actually came from many diverse cultures. Most were English speakers from British Empire colonies such as Jamaica, Trinidad, Barbados, the Virgin Islands, and Bermuda. A few were Haitian French or Creole speakers. Those from Curaçao spoke Dutch, and some from other colonies spoke Spanish. During the 1920s, most of these immigrants maintained separate national clubs and thought of themselves as immigrants rather than as African Americans.

West Indian immigrants arrived in America with a different set of expectations than the Southern black migrants brought with them. They came from majority black countries where one might see white people only rarely and where black people had more autonomy. Skilled construction trades, for example, were open to black Jamaicans but not to African Americans. West Indians were also not used to the insulting behavior of many white Americans, and they were likely to reply in kind. One measure of this combativeness was that the Pullman Company generally did not hire West Indians as porters because porters were expected to endure all kinds of rudeness politely.

Some West Indians, such as the leading black socialist, Virgin Islander Hubert Harrison, held radical labor opinions.

Many immigrants also brought with them an entrepreneurial tradition. In a Jamaican village, the shopkeepers were typically black. This situation contrasted with the American South, where white people usually ran the few stores, especially in small towns. In Harlem, West Indians saved their money, pooled their earnings with fellow countrymen, and opened neighborhood grocery stores. This pattern was typical of all immigrant groups but foreign to black migrants from the oppressive South.

Even religious practices differed between West Indians and African Americans. Since most West Indians came from the British Empire, they typically belonged to the Episcopal Church. Services in that church were more restrained than the emotional services in many African American churches. West Indians might play cricket instead of baseball or socialize with fellows at distinct social clubs. These cultural differences served to consolidate distinct West Indian communities.

The differences between West Indian immigrants and African Americans created some tensions between the two groups during the 1920s. Sometimes they viewed each other skeptically. To West Indians, African Americans might seem too resigned to their outcast status. African Americans might think West Indians too presumptuous and naïve about American race relations. The most visible manifestation of the tensions appeared with the rise of Marcus Garvey's Universal Negro Improvement Association, which we discuss in chapter 5. Garvey, a Jamaican immigrant, won a large following among people of both groups, but some African American critics thought that Garvey misunderstood American race relations. On the other hand, thousands of West Indians and African Americans met in the neighborhood or at work and became friends. And in the next generation, the children of the immigrants often thought of themselves as more generically "black" as they adopted American ways.

As they became increasingly urban, African Americans became a part of the industrial work force. The manufacturing sector, along with transportation and mining, provided employment for 27.2 percent of all black workers. This category included over a million factory workers, four hundred thousand transportation workers (many of them track laborers), and almost seventy-five thousand miners. This development had an important effect upon the workers themselves, their families, and their communities. In general, migration made them more prosperous than they had been in the South. Yet, black workers were typically confined to the bottom of the industrial job ladder, forming a lower caste within the working class. Despite the changes brought by the migration, a majority of black people stayed in traditional occupations. In 1930, 36 percent of all African Americans still worked in agriculture, and 28 percent were in domestic service.

Employment opportunities for African American women were severely curtailed compared with those of both black men and white women. Overwhelmingly, they were confined to working as domestic servants, hotel maids, and kitchen cooks. A 1930 study of black women workers in Chicago found that over 80 percent worked as domestic servants. During World War I, black women obtained some jobs in light industry, working in mail-order houses, garment shops, and food-processing plants. However, as the soldiers came home, the women lost their jobs.

Still, work as a domestic in the North had advantages over work in the South. Many Southern black women continued to work long hours in the fields as sharecroppers' wives and daughters. Maids were very poorly paid in the South. Those who came north, even to work as domestics, improved their situations. In many cities, social service agencies or black women's clubs protected these women from sexual abuse, false accusations of theft, and economic exploitation. In Cleveland, Jane Edna Hunter established the Phillis Wheatley boarding homes for them, and in Boston Melnea Cass championed their cause.

In many Northern industrial cities, black workers brought about several important changes. They raised their own standard of living relative to their previous situations, they formed a new lower caste within the working class, and they confronted white workers, demanding to be treated fairly by their fellow workers. The fact that few blacks returned to their old homes testifies to the fact that the rewards of the migration outweighed the difficulties.

A review of several different situations shows that black people registered real economic gains by migrating north. The steel mills of Pittsburgh attracted thousands of black migrants. The African American population of Pittsburgh and the surrounding industrial Allegheny County more than doubled between 1910 and 1930. Blacks were relatively widely distributed throughout the county because of the dispersal of smaller plants, although Pittsburgh's older black residential sector, the Hill District, remained the most densely populated area. Other black neighborhoods, such as the Ward, an area within walking distance of the massive Homestead Steel Works, also gained in size.

Black male workers in Pittsburgh earned an average of forty to fifty cents per hour for most of the 1920s. This represented a major increase in pay for

Southern migrants. Black workers could buy better food, clothing, shelter, and entertainment for their families. For example, by 1930, 20 percent of blacks in Pittsburgh owned a radio, while only 3 percent of Atlanta black families owned one.

Yet, black workers in Pittsburgh almost always found themselves in the lowest paid and most demanding jobs as compared with white workers. In 1920, 85 percent of black steelworkers were toiling in the blast furnaces or as general laborers wielding picks, shovels, or brooms. Only small numbers of black workers could be found at the skilled trades in the industry. The unskilled men mostly worked together in gangs under an African American foreman, just as white immigrants usually had a bilingual countryman as foreman. The difference was that many immigrants moved up in job category as they acquired English-language and industrial skills and gained seniority. Black workers usually were unable to advance.

White workers tried to exclude blacks from the workplace, and if the plants hired blacks anyway, they often refused to work with them and excluded them from their unions. Not surprisingly, during the great steel strike in the fall of 1919, when thousands of western Pennsylvania workers walked off their jobs, African Americans typically stayed at work, and thousands more rushed to take jobs at the plants. Blacks were even deputized in some towns and patrolled factories with guns. This temporary reversal of power relations left a legacy of bitterness between black and white workers, but it did not result in explosions of violence as it had in Chicago. Thus, Pittsburgh provided economic improvement over the South but not racial harmony in the workplace.

Cleveland was typical of most Northern industrial cities with a more diverse manufacturing base than Pittsburgh. Black workers here had more opportunities for advancement than in Pittsburgh, where they were confined to less-skilled jobs. Between 1910 and 1930, Cleveland's black population rose from 8,488 to 71,889, making it 8 percent black and the twelfth largest African America city. Before World War I, black men worked mostly as servants, with only 22 percent employed in manufacturing. After the war, almost two-thirds of Cleveland's black males worked in industrial occupations, while only 12 percent worked as servants.

Unlike black workers in Pittsburgh, more African Americans were able to secure skilled jobs in Cleveland. For example, one casting plant employed black men as molders, crane operators, melting-furnace operators, and at a variety of similar jobs. They received the same rate of pay as white coworkers, about $20 per week, much more than they would have earned in the South.

By 1920, just over one-fourth of black male Clevelanders, about four thousand, were working in skilled and semiskilled jobs. Their increased purchasing power contributed to the emergence of a black middle class.

More contact with white workers led to better race relations than in Pittsburgh or Chicago, but relations were still strained. Cleveland was one of the few places where African American workers participated in the nationwide 1919 steel strike. But even in the best of situations, white workers showed their hostility. Trade unions in Cleveland typically barred blacks from membership. White restaurant and hotel workers went on strike to drive black employees out of their jobs. Black community leaders struck back. In 1928, when unions tried to pass a national anti-injunction bill limiting the authority of courts in strikes, they testified before a Senate committee, voicing concern that the law would give unions power to bar black workers.

During the 1920s, no city in America changed more than Detroit, both demographically and industrially. Detroit had the fastest rate of black population growth of any major American city in the 1920s. Historically, it had a small, isolated African American population. In 1900, only about four thousand black people lived among almost three hundred thousand whites. But by 1920, that figure had shot up by a factor of ten to almost forty thousand people, and by the end of the decade, it had tripled again. These new arrivals came mostly from Alabama, Georgia, Florida, Arkansas, and Mississippi.

The migrants came to work in Henry Ford's auto plant, the largest industrial employer of African Americans. Ford believed that the black workers would be opposed to unions and loyal to him for giving them a break. Until the end of the Depression, he was right. The automobile industry spawned aluminum and steel fabricating plants, and in other nearby cities, it created glass and rubber industries. Black workers streamed into Detroit to build the cars. By 1926, ten thousand African Americans worked at Detroit's enormous River Rouge Ford plant. They also worked for other companies, too, such as Dodge and Packard. In all these places, black workers took the most demanding and dangerous jobs. They sprayed paint, ground steel, sanded metal, and worked the assembly line.

Black church and community leaders, particularly the Urban League, vetted employees for Ford. To work there, prospective employees needed a letter from their minister or an Urban League official. This led to a close relationship between the black community leaders and the auto industry. Perhaps as a result, black workers did not want to get involved with any labor organizing. The auto plants remained unorganized during the 1920s. It was not until the next decade that unionists challenged the factory owners.

While most black people moved to big cities, many thousands moved to smaller urban areas like Milwaukee, Wisconsin, or mining towns in West Virginia. These places might offer fewer opportunities to find a spouse, but they typically displayed less racial tension. Moreover, black people often formed closer bonds in small black communities. Milwaukee was perhaps typical of these cities, although, like all places, it had its own unique characteristics. The attraction of Chicago and Detroit, with their large black communities and industrial plants, kept the Milwaukee black community relatively small. During the1920s, it more than doubled in size, reaching seventy-five hundred people, scarcely more than 1 percent of the city's total population.

Before the war, Milwaukee's African Americans worked mostly in service jobs, but afterward about three-quarters of the men and two-fifths of the women secured factory jobs. The men could earn up to $5 in an eight-hour workday, almost twice the wage of a factory hand in the South. In Milwaukee, they worked in the iron and steel industries, slaughterhouses, tanneries, and construction. As usual, they worked in the toughest jobs, risking exhaustion in blast furnaces or inhaling toxic fumes in tanneries.

Race relations in Milwaukee should have been better. After all, the city, full of radical German Americans who had recently been the victims of wartime persecution, was a stronghold of socialism. Milwaukee elected a socialist mayor and congressman in the postwar years. While race relations on the job were probably better there than in other cities, even radicals kept the unions white and black workers in the lower-paying jobs.

One unique region in the country was the southern West Virginia coal-mining district. Scores of small towns there provided the manpower to extract the bituminous coal that heated the nation's homes and fired its locomotives. Despite the very real hazards of coal mining, thousands of black people moved there to take advantage of economic opportunities. Migrants to the region came mostly from nearby rural Virginia. They made the shortest journey of all of the migrants but changed their lives as much as those who traveled farther north. Tobacco was Virginia's cash crop, and like cotton, it provided an uncertain economic future. With mine operators appealing for more help, migration to southern West Virginia continued throughout the decade. The black population grew by twenty thousand to reach eighty thousand people by the end of the decade. A quarter of those people worked in the mines.

Black coal miners earned good money, up to $5 for an eight-hour day. Most worked as loaders and were paid by the ton, but the companies also opened some higher-skilled jobs to black workers. Machine operators bought automobiles, saved money, and enjoyed a relatively high standard of living. Yet, all coal miners paid a price. Black lung disease and death by cave-in were occupational hazards in the riskiest job in America.

African Americans made important social gains during the Jazz Age but still lagged far behind whites in their overall quality of life. The most important long-term gain African Americans made was in education. They made sacrifices to send their children to school, seeing education as a new avenue for individual and racial advancement. In the South especially, they had to struggle for access to public education and often created new schools themselves. Over 2.5 million African American children attended school for at least some time during the 1929 school year, about 60 percent of those eligible, compared to a 70 percent white attendance rate. African Americans did not lag too far behind the whites; however, white students stayed in school longer and had better facilities, smaller classes, and better-trained teachers.

Most encouraging of all, there was a sharp decrease in black illiteracy. In 1920, almost a quarter of all black people could not read, but that figure had dropped about 10 percent by the end of the decade. Literacy rates among blacks varied greatly between North and South. The vast majority of illiterate blacks lived in the South. Southern state and county governments appropriated only the barest minimum of funding to black education. No one enforced compulsory education laws for black children. By contrast, illiteracy rates in Northern states were sometimes almost the same for the two races. In Buffalo, New York, for example, fewer than 3 percent of African Americans were illiterate, the same percentage as the white population. In Chattanooga, Tennessee, by comparison, over 11 percent of African Americans were illiterate, more than twice the percentage for whites. Obviously, migration improved educational opportunities.

The migration produced some gender imbalances, especially in the South. African American women had longer life spans than black men in the 1920s. The 1930 census found that there were only 97 black men for every 100 women. Among whites, the figure was 102.7 men per 100 women. Since most migrants were male, because the job opportunities were better for them, the gender imbalance became more heavily female in the South. The shortage of older black men made it harder for widows to remarry. Divorce was uncommon for most Americans in the 1920s, and only about 2 percent of the black population reported that they were divorced, although it is likely that many who claimed to be legally married were separated.

Nonetheless, the migration probably contributed to greater gender equality. African American women gained more reproductive freedom during the 1920s. On one hand, the lack of marriageable men created a hardship for women who desired a spouse. On the other hand, the general shortage of men probably created more autonomy for women. The smaller size of Northern black families suggests that women had more access to, and information about, birth control.

It is important to remember that the typical African American family of the 1920s lived in the rural South. Here, much remained the same as in earlier decades. Black people mostly worked as tenant farmers or sharecroppers on land owned by whites. They toiled for long hours in oppressive weather, were often cheated out of a fair price for their crops, enjoyed no civil rights, and had to defer to whites. African Americans gradually left the farm during the decade, and the total value of their agricultural property declined.

African Americans ran 14 percent of all farms in the United States, slightly more than their percentage of the total population. They lived hard lives. Only 16 percent owned their own land; 45 percent were sharecroppers and the rest were tenant farmers. Almost all of these farmers lived in the South. In the "Black Belt," the lower Mississippi River valley, and the east-west strip of central Alabama, African Americans operated three-fourths of all farms and about half the farms in the South Carolina Piedmont. Almost none of these farmers had electricity, a telephone, or running water. They used mules to pull their wagons and plows. About half had some pigs or cows, probably mostly for home consumption. These black farmers raised about 30 percent of the nation's cotton, 25 percent of the sweet potatoes, and 16 percent of the corn for grain. Most of them grew cotton. Yet, white owners claimed much of the money for their crops as rent or payment for startup capital, such as the buildings, mules, fertilizer, and tools.

For many rural blacks, the decline of agriculture in the 1920s was a real disaster. Many people at the bottom of the economic ladder fell into various forms of peonage, or debt slavery. Sharecroppers were often told at harvest time that they still owed money to the landowner and, therefore, could not leave the land. A landlord acting as cotton broker could lie about the market value of the cotton, the cost of interest on his debt, or anything else, and the sharecropper had no recourse but to toil without pay for another year. A young black man could get arrested for "vagrancy" if the police found him without any cash in his pockets. Then, he could be imprisoned until an unscrupulous white farmer bailed him out and then held him as a laborer. Some convicts were leased out to road builders, who might drive their labor unmercifully on a chain gang. Debt peonage was illegal under federal law, but this law was rarely enforced in the South. The practice was kept quiet and was probably fairly widespread.

Two horrific events in 1921 illustrated the desperate situations in which rural black people often found themselves. Henry Lowry, a tenant farmer from Nodena, Arkansas, in the Mississippi Delta, was cheated out of a fair settlement on his crop. When the armed Lowry confronted his landlord, a gunfight broke out in which Lowry was wounded and two whites killed. Lowry fled to Texas, where he was arrested and returned to Arkansas by train. A lynch mob, most likely in collusion with the lawmen, intercepted the train, and Lowry was burnt at the stake. The lynching was advertised in advance, a large crowd attended the ghastly execution, and no effort was made to arrest the perpetrators. Lowry's plight showed the helpless situation of most African American tenant farmers and sharecroppers.

Later in the year, a white farmer in Jasper County, Georgia, was accused of murdering black workers on his farm. Eleven bodies were discovered in two counties. The victims were men who had been bailed out of prison by farmer John Williams and then worked like slaves on his farm. When one of the prisoners escaped and told federal investigators of the situation, Williams killed the remaining men to prevent them from testifying and threw the bodies into a river. At the trial, he blamed his African American foreman for the atrocities, but an all-white jury convicted him. John Williams became the first white man convicted for the murder of a black man since Reconstruction. He was sentenced to life in prison and died there. The Williams "murder farm" case made headline news and highlighted the problem of prison laborers forced to work on private farms. However, the case was treated as an aberration, and the economic exploitation of rural Southern blacks remained a problem for many years.

The Lowry and Williams cases demonstrate the harshness of Southern race relations during the 1920s. Southern African Americans made some gains in education and increased their presence in Southern cities, but few rural blacks could improve their situation in those years, except by leaving for the North. The migration to the North was therefore the most important development of the time, even though only a minority of black people left the South. The migration North changed the face of black America and offered all African Americans the first real hope they had had since the Reconstruction era.

~

CHAPTER THREE

Changing Institutions in Changing Times

A central dilemma of African American life has been how best to resolve the tension between the struggle for full equality and the desire to maintain ethnic identity, a difficulty made unique for African Americans by the history of slavery and segregation. In the first half of the twentieth century, the problem was this: would African Americans' building their own institutions signal to whites that they would not insist on admission to "white" institutions? For the most part, black people had few choices. White Americans did not allow black people into their churches, businesses, unions, schools, hospitals, or anywhere else. Blacks would have to develop a separate, parallel set of institutions. The migration and the growth of urban communities in the North made the 1920s a time of black institution building. African Americans built churches, businesses, labor unions, women's clubs, schools, professional associations, newspapers, and other institutions. The confidence they gained in building these separate institutions gave them the courage to speak out for civil rights.

During the 1920s, white people fought among themselves over contrasting notions of gender, social class, ethnicity, religion, and other matters. Black people had a very different experience. Because the prejudices of white society bore down so heavily on all black people, tensions within the black community were muted. For example, few black men argued against the notion that black women should vote. Black workers in black-owned businesses probably never went on strike. Almost all African Americans were Protestant, but few harbored anti-Catholic sentiment at a time when white Protestants joined the Ku Klux Klan and threatened their Catholic neighbors.

Tensions existed, to be sure, but in contrast to whites, African Americans were bound together by a common experience and knowledge of common oppression. This situation made institution building easier. Old and new black institutions flourished in the 1920s.

The most important institution in the African American community had always been the church, and this remained true even during the wild "Roaring Twenties." Like the white churches, the African American denominations were concerned mainly with the salvation of individual souls and the teaching of Christian behavior. But the black church had always been different, and not just in its liturgy or fervor of singing and preaching. The black church served as a social center and meeting place for civic functions, as well as a provider of welfare and education. Excluded from most institutions, millions of black people centered their community life on their churches.

The African American church showed similarities to and differences from white Protestant denominations. Baptists and Methodists, in various denominations, made up the majority of American Christians of both races. Their prayers and hymns were often quite similar. The religious content of the sermons might also be similar, for sin and redemption are universal themes. But Christianity always had a special resonance for African Americans. They believed in an activist, all-powerful God who punished wicked oppressors and brought justice to this world, not just the next. They could hear, in the story of Christ, a story like their own. Black congregations listened to the Old Testament story of the Jewish escape from bondage with great enthusiasm. They knew more about oppression and suffering than white Americans, and they showed great emotion as they retold biblical stories in prayer and song.

Despite the shared Christianity of whites and African Americans, congregations did not communicate across the racial divide. Black and white ministers rarely met in interracial fellowship, and their denominations had separate governing boards. White ministers probably often knew their local black colleagues, but white Baptists and black Baptists lived in two different worlds, although sometimes the racial barriers would come down. Charitable works occasioned by natural disaster, such as the Mississippi River flood of 1927, brought out the best in many Christians. But few black people ever set foot in a "white" church, and few whites ever attended service at an African Methodist Episcopal service. Sunday morning was the most segregated hour in segregated America.

The number of black churches and church members grew throughout the 1920s. A 1926 census of religious bodies found twenty-four African American denominations. They had 37,790 church buildings, almost 90 percent of which were in the South. Over five million people were members of these congregations. Women anchored these churches, outnumbering men by a ratio of ten to six.

The largest denominations were the Baptists. Following a quarrel over control of the Baptist publishing board, the body split in 1915 into two churches called the National Baptist Convention, U.S.A., and the National Baptist Convention of America. Other denominations also employed the name "Baptist" in their titles. The census reported that together they accounted for about 60 percent of all black church members, with approximately three million members. Baptist hierarchies did not impose control over member churches, which had a great deal of autonomy. During the 1920s, the most prominent Baptist-sponsored black colleges were Benedict College in Columbia, South Carolina; Virginia Union University in Richmond, Virginia; Shaw University in Raleigh, North Carolina; and Morehouse and Spelman in Atlanta, Georgia.

Four Methodist denominations accounted for roughly another 30 percent of parishioners in 1926. These were, in size order, the African Methodist Episcopal, African Methodist Episcopal Zion, Methodist Episcopal, and Colored Methodist Episcopal churches. The Methodist churches also sponsored colleges, among which the best known was Wilberforce in Ohio. The remaining 10 percent of black congregants attended a variety of churches.

The African American church changed with changing demographic patterns during the 1920s. Some Southern congregations dwindled, while the expansion of the Northern population led to a geographic reconfiguration of each city's religious community. As old churches were abandoned and bigger buildings were acquired in new neighborhoods, migrants contributed to building funds for the new churches. With a wider choice of churches, class distinctions became more apparent. Most importantly, especially for those who had relocated, the church provided a gathering place for people trying to make their way in a new and confusing place.

The most visible change was the appearance of new buildings. In Cleveland, for example, the city's 44 black churches mushroomed to over 140 by 1933. One Alabama church moved its entire congregation to Cleveland. In Harlem, the Salem Memorial Mission began in its pastor's living room in 1902. In 1923 it purchased a magnificent building from a wealthy white congregation. In Philadelphia, new congregations bought formerly white-owned buildings in North Central and West Philadelphia.

For some cities, the migration led to a consolidation of the black community and the need for the black churches to move to a new location. Harlem typified this phenomenon. The Abyssinian Baptist Church, led by the Reverend Adam Clayton Powell, Sr., led the way uptown, making its plans as early as 1911. Other congregations followed suit, sponsoring "On to Harlem" fund drives. As new congregants made it hard to get a seat on Sunday, churches sped up their moving plans, hoping to avoid rising real estate costs. The new churches soon became landholders themselves, offering their parishioners apartments at low rates. St. Philip's Protestant Episcopal, once a poor downtown congregation, became the most exclusive black church in New York and an important Harlem landlord.

The new churches brought about an increased class consciousness within the black community. A family's church membership indicated its economic and social standing. People of higher income might feel that a storefront building was no longer an appropriate venue from which to offer their prayers. Lower-income people might feel locked out of the impressive new buildings whose construction and maintenance required parishioners with healthy pocketbooks. Moreover, Sunday services at "high-class" and storefront churches differed. St. Philip's Episcopal, for example, might feature a learned sermon and restrained hymns. At storefront churches, new migrants from the South shouted "Amen!" when the preacher touched their souls and belted out hymns to the percussion of a tambourine. Thus, as parishioners gained greater choice of denomination, a new sense of class status emerged within the black community.

Other important institutions of the black community were the Young Men's and Young Women's Christian Associations (YMCA and YWCA). Racially separate branches of the "Y" had existed since their founding in the mid-nineteenth century. The YMCA's motto was to develop "the whole man—body, mind, and spirit," and it offered athletic, cultural, and religious programs that were readily accessible. Its Christian framework and social work orientation naturally raised the contradictory nature of race segregation within the Y. As New Negroes became more assertive, they fought to desegregate the YMCA, or at least to direct their own programs.

The leader of the separate YMCAs had been William Alpheus Hunton, who died in 1916. Mindful of the postwar mood, black YMCA leaders of the 1920s, such as Jesse E. Moorland and Channing Tobias, argued for desegregation of the branches without any success. At the Y's segregated camps in North Carolina, Moorland and Tobias encouraged interracial meetings among youth leaders. However, whites did not permit interracial social arrangements at the camps. The black leaders refused to attend meetings on these terms, and progress toward desegregation within the Y stalled. Moorland and Tobias, however, did convince white leaders to place African American representatives on metropolitan YMCA councils in some Northern cities.

The YMCAs became bedrock institutions in most black urban communities. They organized athletic leagues, educational classes, poetry readings, lectures, and social affairs. By the end of the 1920s, thirty-four thousand African Americans belonged to separate Y branches, thirty-six of which owned buildings. In many black communities, the YMCA played a crucial role in establishing that community's character.

A few white YMCA leaders in the South tried to mitigate worsening race relations after the war. Willis Duke Weatherford, who had founded the YMCA leadership training school in Blue Ridge, North Carolina, promoted the idea of a school dedicated to interracial dialogue. He would not, however, violate norms of segregation, and African American YMCA leaders would not submit to humiliating conditions within their own organization. Because of this stalemate, Atlanta YMCA leaders established a Commission on Interracial Cooperation (CIC) with a leadership training school for African Americans at Gammon Theological Seminary.

The commission's leader during the 1920s was Will W. Alexander, a white YMCA official who worked to improve the conditions of life for African Americans, encourage dialogue, end lynching, and ease racial tensions. The CIC published a monthly bulletin with articles on modern farming, health, and education. It lobbied Southern governments to provide better schools, libraries, parks, and other facilities in black communities. The group did not challenge white supremacy, but few whites espoused its racial uplift goals in the 1920s. Although W. E. B. DuBois and other civil rights activists sometimes expressed impatience with the CIC's reluctance to speak out against segregation, the organization played its part in changing the harsh Southern racial climate. By the end of the decade, the CIC had helped to establish a tradition of moderate white racial liberalism that allowed space for the emergence of the black-led civil rights movement and for white moderates in the clergy and press.

African Americans also built new businesses and expanded old ones during the 1920s. The growth of black urban communities facilitated the development of black-owned insurance companies, banks, real estate companies, retail outlets, and other operations. Grocery stores, pharmacies, barbershops, and other service providers created downtown business districts that stabilized black communities. Though marginal in the overall American economy, these businesses gave millions of people hope that the American dream might be open to them as well. In the short term, that hope proved false. The decline of the economy in the late 1920s, even before the stock market crash of 1929, wiped out black businesspeople first. By the 1930s, only the strongest and most conservative black businesses survived.

Black-owned financial and insurance institutions grew out of fraternal lodges that functioned as cooperatives that enabled poor people to purchase life insurance and burial plots. By the 1920s, millions of African Americans could obtain these services, as well as a mortgage, business loan, or commercial fire-insurance policies from black-owned institutions. The country's largest black-owned business during the 1920s grew out of an alliance between a barber and the Duke family tobacco barons in Durham, North Carolina. The North Carolina Mutual Life Insurance Company operated in eleven states and the District of Columbia, employing over fifteen hundred employees. It helped organize the National Negro Insurance Association (NNIA) in 1921. Led by the company's Charles Clinton Spaulding, the NNIA claimed forty-two member companies, becoming black America's most important economic institution. Another spin-off of the parent company was the Bankers Fire Insurance Company, which made it possible for black businesses to purchase fire insurance, and another company wrote commercial loans. Without these financial institutions to back them, many black entrepreneurs could not have made a start.

A more spectacular, but unhappy, story was that of Herman Perry and the Standard Life Insurance Company of Georgia, which employed twenty-five hundred people and also operated in many states. Perry expanded into construction, fuel delivery, real estate, laundry, printing, and pharmacy companies. When Standard Life collapsed in 1925, it took the rest of the business empire with it. Alonzo F. Herndon's Atlanta Mutual Company probably picked up much of the business Perry lost. Born a slave, Herndon left an estate valued at over half a million dollars when he died in 1927.

Financial institutions in the North were newer and did not originate from fraternal lodges. In Chicago, Jesse Binga organized the Binga State Bank. He had been a barber, Pullman porter, fruit peddler, and real estate man before going into banking. He built the largest black-owned bank in the country, but questionable real estate lending practices led to his making bad loans, some to his own dummy corporations. The bank failed in the 1930s, and he was convicted of bank fraud. Anthony Overton founded the Douglass National Bank, also in Chicago. His initial capital came from a cosmetics business. He later expanded into real estate, life insurance, publishing, and other ventures. The Douglass Bank, like many banks, failed during the Depression. By the 1940s, only six black-owned banks were operating. The flourishing of these businesses during the 1920s marks the period as a golden age of black entrepreneurship.

African Americans initiated or improved construction and real estate projects as well. The Windham Brothers Construction Company in Birmingham, Alabama, began by building homes in the black community. After a few years, they accepted contracts from whites. Similar businesses appeared in Florida, Maryland, and Virginia. Black engineers and builders put up important buildings, such as the Walnut Plaza Apartments in Philadelphia and several medical buildings in New York. The most important realtors of the day were those who developed Harlem. Beginning at the turn of the century, by the 1920s Henry C. Parker and John Nail, along with St. Philips Protestant Episcopal Church, were among the biggest landlords in Harlem.

Black people established a wider variety of companies in the 1920s than they had before. Perhaps the best known was Madame C. J. Walker's beauty-products company. Born Sarah Breedlove in 1867 to Louisiana tenant farmers, she was orphaned as a child and spent her early years as a St. Louis washerwoman. Breedlove developed a hair-treatment process involving hot combs and ointments, and by 1910 she had established a company headquarters in Indianapolis. The legendary Madame C. J. Walker, as she renamed herself, became a millionaire, and her business employed thousands of salespeople, mostly women, throughout the 1920s. C. R. Patterson and Sons Carriage Company of Greenfield, Ohio, manufactured truck and school bus bodies. Black businesspeople managed a cottonseed mill in Mound Bayou, Mississippi, a clothing factory in Ocala, Florida, and New York's Berry and Ross doll factory, which produced black dolls.

Beside these high profile businesses, over twenty-five thousand black-owned stores sold retail goods. They provided a variety of services, which formed the core of downtown business districts in black communities. Many towns had a black-owned grocery store, restaurant, drug store, ice cream parlor, clothing shop, or tobacco stand. Service providers like barbers, beauticians, or doctors and dentists added to the mix. These places made a town feel like "home" to everyone who lived there. Often the proprietor knew all his patrons by name, and his or her waiting room was a venue for exchanging news and gossip. These businesses made up a separate black economy, sheltered from white competitors by an expanding black community. If they were marginal in relation to white-owned enterprises, they nevertheless suggested that black people, too, could succeed in business.

An important social service agency that assisted blacks in their efforts to find employment was the Urban League. Founded in 1910 by African American social workers, community leaders, and white philanthropists, the Urban League was a product of the settlement house movement that sought to help European immigrants secure jobs and housing. Black leaders realized that Southern migrants needed the same services that immigrants did. The Urban League's key leaders during the 1920s were Eugene Kinckle Jones, the executive secretary; Charles S. Johnson, editor of *Opportunity*, its magazine; and T. Arnold Hill, director of industrial relations. The Urban League functioned as a service agency, not a membership organization that solicited recruits. Wealthy whites contributed the money. Most of its branches were in the North and Midwest, and although it tried to expand in the South, it had little luck there. Nevertheless, it was extremely important in the reshaping of black America. It helped open doors to work that previously had been shut to black employees.

The United States had no laws prohibiting employment discrimination in the 1920s. Urban League officials approached white employers who did not hire blacks and tried to persuade them to change their hiring policies. They pointed to successful ventures, such as Henry Ford's auto plants, and offered them as a model. They argued that manufacturers who hired African Americans could expect to sell their products in the black community. The Boston Urban League got jobs for black workers in hotels and at the Gillette razor blade factory. In Chicago, black workers at International Harvester and Western Union owed their jobs to the Urban League's efforts. The Urban League also trained migrants for industrial jobs. It ran adult education courses for various trades, promoted health education and child welfare, and did social work. It claimed to have assisted forty thousand people in finding employment annually during the 1920s. Even if that figure is inflated, the Urban League clearly helped migrants to establish themselves in the North.

Institutions such as the Urban League were especially important given the state of African American unions. The American Federation of Labor, which nominally was committed to the brotherhood of all workers, allowed its affiliates to bar blacks from membership and, hence, employment almost everywhere that it had contracts. White workers regarded blacks as a permanent underclass, a threat to the good wages that white people earned. White workers put their race prejudice ahead of their class solidarity, thus weakening the labor movement.

This attitude produced a feeling of suspicion and hostility toward labor unions among black workers. In general, African American community lead-

ers viewed themselves as honest brokers between white employers and prospective black employees. This was a central theme of Booker T.
Washington's 1895 Atlanta speech in which he urged employers to hire African Americans rather than immigrants in the South's emerging industries.
Some employers, like Henry Ford, worked with Detroit's black community
leaders to hire people whom they had vetted. Black workers might have their
own inevitable problems with management once they were hired, but it was
not until late in the Depression of the 1930s that African Americans and
labor unions made their first, often bumpy, approaches toward one another.

In most industries that employed African Americans (auto, steel, packinghouse, or shipping), either there were no unions or black people had just
a few scattered members among their ranks. Only on the railroad was there
a tradition of independent African American organization. The railroad
industry was unique in several respects. First of all, on any one carrier, the
workers were divided among themselves by as many as fourteen craft unions.
These were in turn divided, especially in the South, by race. Whites occupied the higher-skilled jobs such as engineer, dispatcher, block operator, or
conductor. More arduous jobs, like building and maintaining the tracks, or
servile jobs, like cooking for and assisting passengers, were reserved for African Americans. Some jobs that were dangerous or better paying used workers
of both races, who could "bid" on individual jobs but only on seniority lists
separated by color; these jobs included work as firemen, who stoked the
engine's boilers with coal; brakemen, who coupled and uncoupled cars to
make a train; or switchmen, who worked in yards throwing switches. Com-
plicating this picture was the fact that employers often preferred black workers, whose lack of rights in society made them less militant than white
workers. During the 1920s, there was no national highway system, and the
large truck had not yet been developed. Most of the nation's freight and
interstate passengers traveled by rail. Thus, railroad strikes could cripple the
American economy.

These precariously balanced racial and labor relations began to come
apart in the post–World War I labor upsurge. During the war, the Woodrow
Wilson administration had established governing boards for American industry to keep the economy running smoothly. After the war, business leaders
felt that labor had gained the advantage, and they were now determined to
reassert control. In this context, white railroad workers demanded that they
get jobs held by black workers on several railroads in the border states and
the Mississippi River valley. They resorted to an unauthorized strike, and by
the end of 1919, they had taken hundreds of jobs held by black workers. In

Mississippi, this campaign was accompanied by a wave of murder and beatings. In 1921 the corpse of Horace Hurd was found on the tracks with a note pinned to it: "Let this be a lesson to all nigger brakemen."

African American workers fought back, but their organizations were too weak to prevail. Their first union, the Railwaymen's International Benevolent Industrial Association, led by Robert L. Mays, had a membership of fifteen thousand by 1920. The American Federation of Labor ostracized them, and they won no contracts. Another group, headquartered in Memphis and led by John Henry Eiland, the Colored Association of Railroad Employees, appealed to the Railway Labor Board on behalf of the victimized workers. The board turned down their plea in 1925, and black men disappeared from skilled jobs involving train operations in the South.

Both of these black labor organizations sought to cooperate with the carriers. Their failure laid the groundwork for a new approach by militant unionists who worked as Pullman porters. These jobs were among the best and most visible held by black people in the United States. The Pullman Company employed twelve thousand porters, almost all of whom were African American. Pullman won a great deal of support in the community for hiring these men. In addition, the company bought friends in the black press by purchasing advertisements, and it contributed to hospitals and other community institutions.

Nevertheless, wages for porters were low, hours long, and conditions bad. Porters were always on call, subject to the whims of fussy white passengers, dependent upon them for tips, and always blamed whenever passengers complained. They were not paid for traveling to work or returning to base if a job ended away from home. Union organizers could be fired at will, like everybody else. The Pullman porters organized a union, the Brotherhood of Sleeping Car Porters, to change these conditions. In 1925, three porters approached A. Philip Randolph and asked him to take charge of the organizing drive.

Born in 1889, Randolph grew up the son of a poor preacher in Jacksonville, Florida. He came to New York in 1911, defraying his ship fare by washing dishes. In New York, he worked as a switchboard operator and attended City College at night. He married a wealthy woman, Lucille Green, who worked with Madame C. J. Walker's cosmetics company. She supported Randolph's work as editor of the *Hotel Messenger*, the voice of the hotel workers' union. The magazine later separated from the union and appeared as *The Messenger* from 1917 to 1924. Randolph and coeditor Chandler Owen championed racial equality, labor rights, and socialism. But as the country prospered in the 1920s, Randolph developed a more pragmatic line, which facilitated his alliance with the Pullman porters. Once a socialist agitator, Randolph now adjusted to the narrower, but crucial, domain of union politics.

Randolph, an unflappable man of dignified bearing and solid character, waged a tireless campaign to win union recognition for the porters. He could not be fired because he was not a porter himself and, hence, was more secure than his predecessors. The company fought back by threatening suspected activists and refusing to negotiate. To protect the men from company spies, Randolph conducted the first organizing meeting, in his magnificent baritone voice, entirely by himself, although hundreds were in attendance. The porters' fight challenged not just the Pullman Company but some black community leaders who thought that African Americans should stay away from labor unions. Some editors of African American newspapers, like Robert Abbott of the *Chicago Defender*, criticized Randolph for attacking the Pullman Company, which bought advertising space in his paper. But the Brotherhood of Sleeping Car Porters, despite many setbacks, finally won recognition in 1935. The union became an important institution in the black community, and Randolph became one of the most prominent black leaders during the 1930s.

Just as a "New Negro" appeared in the 1920s, so too did a "New Woman." African American women participated separately from white women in the suffrage movement. They formed their own contingent in the antilynching struggle, calling on white women to admit that the stereotype of the black male as a rapist was a lie. African American women also emerged as educational leaders by building schools for their younger sisters.

Women had been struggling for the right to vote since the Seneca Falls convention of 1848. By the time of World War I, white women were divided into two rival groups, the National American Women's Suffrage Association (NAWSA) and the direct-action-oriented National Women's Party. Women's participation on the home front during the war convinced President Woodrow Wilson to drop his opposition to women's suffrage. After seventy years of struggle, a women's suffrage amendment finally passed the House of Representatives. In 1919, the bill came before the Senate.

Southern senators attempted to change the wording of the amendment so that the states, rather than Washington, would enforce the new federal amendment. Their intent was to permit white women to vote but block African American women. The National Association of Colored Women (NACW), led by Mary Talbert, Mary Church Terrell, Mary McLeod

Bethune, and others, demanded that white suffragists speak up for black women as voters. The white suffrage leaders, fearing that a forthright stand would lead to the amendment's defeat, gave evasive and unsatisfactory answers. To force the issue, the Northeast Federation of the NACW, led by Elizabeth C. Carter of New Bedford, Massachusetts, applied for membership in the NAWSA. The white suffragists begged Carter to withdraw the application. Carter countered by agreeing, but only on the condition that NAWSA insist on the original language of the amendment. Both groups of white suffragists refused. Nevertheless, the suffrage amendment passed the Senate without the states' rights language and, after a dramatic battle, was ratified in the final state, Tennessee, by one vote in the legislature.

Black women would put their newly won rights to the test in the 1920 election. Mary Church Terrell worked for the Republican National Committee to turn out the new voters. Black women registered throughout the country, even in some Southern cities like New Orleans, Atlanta, and Richmond. But in most Southern places, they were turned away by threats of violence or trickery. In Columbia, South Carolina, where voters had to be taxpayers, determined black women showed up, holding the proper receipts. The registrars simply put the black women at the end of the line and kept them waiting all day as white people registered. The following day, the women came back. This time the sheriff threatened to shoot them. Undaunted, the women swore out affidavits against the local authorities, and in December, the National Association for the Advancement of Colored People (NAACP) presented them to Congress as evidence that Southern whites were defying the Constitution.

African American women next pressed the National Women's Party to join the fight. Alice Paul, the militant leader of that group, discouraged them. Her position was that they were raising a question of race, not gender discrimination, which, strictly speaking, was true. But Paul evaded the real issue of gender solidarity. Sixty black women attended the 1921 convention of the National Women's Party. They put forward a resolution calling for a federal investigation into the disfranchisement of black women. The resolution failed, but the petitioners had raised a central strategic point: "No women are free until all women are free," the resolution insisted.

Black women's struggle for the vote uplifted all African Americans. In a similar fashion, black women played a special role in the effort to pass the Dyer Antilynching Bill during 1922. The preeminent figure in this historic struggle had been Ida B. Wells. After reporting about the 1892 lynching of three black Memphis grocers in her newspaper, Wells was forced to flee the

South and take up residence in Chicago. There she helped found the National Association of Colored Women's Clubs (NACW) and, later, the NAACP. For thirty years, Wells argued against the racist myth at the heart of white fears: that black men wanted to rape white women. Wells showed that such acts were extremely rare and that most interracial rapists were white men whose crimes went unpunished. Wells remained an independent activist in the 1920s, but new groups took up her torch.

In 1922, Mary B. Talbert launched the Antilynching Crusaders to back the campaign for the Dyer bill. The women organized fund-raising events, contributed money, and distributed literature. By organizing separately as women, they pushed the gender dimension of lynching to the fore. Their intent was to reach out to white women and challenge them to take a stand. Some white women, led by Jessie Daniel Ames of East Texas, did speak out against lynching. The lone Southern vote for the Dyer bill would come from her region. While the bill did not pass, the fight for it contributed to the decline of lynching during the 1920s.

Besides struggling for the vote and against lynching, African American women enhanced their own institutions during the 1920s. The NACW, founded in 1895, addressed wider concerns of black women. During the war, clubwomen organized support and comfort for their sons and brothers in uniform by providing food, clothing, and entertainment for the soldiers. These clubs performed social work for the sick, handicapped, elderly, and other vulnerable people. They promoted cultural activities that gave women a voice and enriched the whole community.

Their most important activity was to promote education for young women. Mary McLeod Bethune, who served as NACW president for much of the decade, epitomized these efforts. Born the fifteenth of seventeen children to a poor family that valued education, she attended mission schools on a scholarship and became a teacher. By 1900, at age twenty-five, she had founded a school at Palatka, Florida. Four years later, she started another, and by the 1920s, her school in Daytona became the Bethune-Cookman College, which enrolled hundreds of female students. She also founded a hospital and school for delinquent girls. As president of the NACW, Bethune established a national headquarters for the organization. Later, she would help initiate the National Council of Negro Women, befriend Eleanor Roosevelt, and advise President Franklin Delano Roosevelt during the New Deal.

Three other women's careers help illuminate the central role women played in establishing educational and community institutions during the 1920s. Charlotte Hawkins Brown was born in North Carolina and raised in

Massachusetts. She returned to her birth state and founded the Palmer Memorial Institute in Sedalia, transforming it into a high school during the 1920s. Nannie Burroughs launched the National Training School for Women and Girls in Washington, D.C., in 1911 as part of the National Baptist Convention. By the 1920s, she was admitting students from across the United States. Burroughs participated actively in the NAACP and the NACW during a long career of service. Lugenia Burns Hope played a similar role in social work. She started the Atlanta Neighborhood Union, which sponsored educational, cultural, health, and neighborhood-cleanup projects. Her pioneering organizational model was followed in other cities. Like her sister educators, Hope served in the NACW. For all of them, advancement of African American women was a crucial part of the freedom struggle during the 1920s.

Most black Americans also saw education as part of the struggle for racial advancement. Very few African Americans attended college during the 1920s, but many of those who did would become the leaders of their communities for the next thirty or forty years. African American higher education had been a contentious issue within the black leadership for decades. From 1895 until his death in 1915, Booker T. Washington, principal at Alabama's Tuskegee Institute, had been the leading spokesperson for manual and technical training. In 1903, W. E. B. DuBois, in *The Souls of Black Folk*, made the case that African Americans should study the same subjects white people did and not relegate themselves to second-class status as students and intellectuals.

By the 1920s, the question had clearly been settled in DuBois's favor. The changing mood among African Americans and the modernization of education led to the demise of the idea that black colleges should focus on technical training. Student revolts during the 1920s, one at Fisk University, DuBois's alma mater, and another at Hampton University, where Washington had been a student, demonstrated the changing mood. Henceforth, black colleges would not only be central institutions of the black community but pillars of the emerging black middle class and trainers of civil rights activists.

Three-quarters of the 13,860 black college students in America during the 1926–1927 school year attended private schools. Yet, very few students at the twenty-three state-funded African American schools were actually taking college-level courses. The private schools were almost exclusively the projects of religious denominations, such as the Methodist Episcopal Church, the American Baptist Home Missionary Society, the Presbyterians, and the

African Methodist Episcopal Church. There were also some interdenominational schools sponsored by the American Missionary Association and others. Some black colleges dated back to the Reconstruction era, and all reflected that period's missionary impulse to further Christianize the freed people. The colleges trained doctors, teachers, ministers, and other professionals. Three of the schools emerged as elite institutions: Fisk in Nashville, Howard in the nation's capital, and Atlanta University.

The key struggle took place at Fisk, sparked by a change in the source of funding for the black college. During Reconstruction, financial contributors had been religious abolitionists. When the reform impulse faded and commercial influence grew, charitable funding through the churches declined. In its place came a more powerful revenue stream, one that came with strings attached. White entrepreneurs like John D. Rockefeller, Julius Rosenwald, William H. Baldwin, George Foster Peabody, and Andrew Carnegie contributed millions to the endowments of black colleges. As white racists consolidated political control in the South, a conservative model for black education took hold. The manual training colleges, such as Hampton Institute in Virginia or Tuskegee, prepared black youth for modest careers as independent farmers, tradesmen, nurses, or elementary school teachers.

By the 1920s, black students and their parents had rejected this model. Black students and educators recognized the need for a revamped system to promote a black leadership class. Even Booker T. Washington's replacement at Tuskegee, Robert F. Moton, showed that he understood the changing mood. To regain what they perceived as their waning influence, the industrial philanthropists announced a campaign to raise $2.5 million each for Hampton and Tuskegee, and $1 million for Fisk.

The money for Fisk was intended to transform the school from a liberal arts college to an industrial training school. Since the school's endowment was microscopic, and the buildings were crumbling, the new donors had a lot of leverage. They changed the board of trustees, who reflected the school's egalitarian past, which had nurtured the young DuBois. The new school president, Fayette A. McKenzie, was fully committed to an industrial training curriculum. He dissolved the student government, muzzled the newspaper, and imposed a restrictive code of student behavior. With these measures, McKenzie consolidated his backing from the philanthropists. The Nashville city fathers, who feared the rise of an independent black institution in their midst, gave their approval as well.

The students, alumni, and African American intelligentsia rose up in revolt. DuBois delivered the 1924 commencement address and stoutly defended Fisk's traditions. Alumni bombarded the trustees with calls for McKenzie's removal. In 1925 the students went on strike, rallying the Nashville black community behind them. DuBois damned the millionaires and praised the student revolt in a ringing editorial. Under this pressure, the trustees backed down. They appointed a more diplomatic president, who conciliated both sides. After some hesitation, the philanthropists, to their credit, made good on their pledges, even though they had relinquished a measure of control.

A somewhat similar process unfolded at Howard University during the 1920s. Founded in 1867 as a theological seminary, Howard was the outstanding black college in the 1920s, but it too suffered low morale under paternalist leadership. After a student strike in 1925, the trustees appointed the school's first black president. Mordecai Johnson had been educated at many colleges, including Harvard and Gammon Theological Seminary. Johnson served as pastor at Charleston, West Virginia's First Baptist Church and participated vigorously in the city's NAACP chapter. He raised morale and set the college on a course that expanded its undergraduate and professional training programs. During the 1920s, literary critic Alain Locke and sociologist Kelly Miller were among the leading lights of Howard's faculty. In the 1930s, its law school produced the lawyers who would challenge segregation in the courts.

During the 1920s, President John Hope built Morehouse College into a third top-tier institution. Born in Georgia and educated at Brown University, Hope became the first black president of Atlanta Baptist College, later Morehouse, in 1906. He recruited such leading scholars as Benjamin Brawley, Samuel Howard Archer, Benjamin Mays, Nathaniel Tillman, and Samuel M. Nabrit. Backed financially by the Rockefeller-funded General Education Board, Hope tripled the enrollment and added new buildings. In 1929 Hope became president of Atlanta University, which united Morehouse, the women's college, Spelman, and new graduate schools, including a pioneering school of social work.

Beside student radicalism, a second factor contributed to the transformation of African American higher education. During the 1920s, many states modernized their standards for teacher training, requiring more classes in academic fields. Hampton and Tuskegee, the flagship schools for the industrial training model, could not meet these standards. Its graduates found themselves unemployable as teachers. By 1927, the Hampton students went on strike, demanding classes that would qualify them for work in a modern economy. Two years later the board changed presidents, giving the new leader a mandate to improve the faculty and curriculum. The rebellion at Hampton definitively ended the notion that black education should focus exclusively on trade school–level training.

As the quality of higher education for African Americans rose during the 1920s, so did the numbers of black professionals. They also found it necessary to develop their own institutions. Nothing dramatized the fundamental problem posed by segregation more than the exclusion of black medical professionals from white-run institutions. Black doctors, nurses, and dentists could not work in white-run medical facilities. This situation meant that African Americans had to build their own separate hospitals, medical schools, professional associations, and journals. Moreover, black patients could not get treatment at white-owned facilities. In emergencies, they died needlessly.

An unusual white attempt to control the Tuskegee Veteran's Adminstration Hospital in 1923 showed the importance of black control of black institutions. When the Veteran's Administration located the black hospital facility in Tuskegee, the Ku Klux Klan mobilized to insist that whites run and staff the hospital. The Klan feared the presence of any black people whose paychecks came from out of state and who would serve as models of competence and independent thinking for the wider community. Moreover, they wanted the jobs for whites. The Klan issued death threats to black personnel at the hospital and staged a menacing march through town. Yet, the Klan's extreme racism put it in the unfamiliar and uncomfortable position of asserting that white doctors and nurses would treat black patients. Even other segregationists recoiled. Civil rights groups and black doctors insisted on black control of the facility. In the face of black unity and white dissension, the federal government put black administrators in charge. The incident showed not just the absurdity of segregation but also the need for black professionals to defend their own skills and prerogatives.

The Tuskegee fight caused black doctors to launch a National Hospital Association in 1923. Thirty-three hospitals joined, all of them black run, although the group was open to any facility that treated black patients. Its first leaders were President H. M. Green, Vice President Joseph H. Ward, and John A. Kenney. The segregated National Medical Association, founded in 1895, had two thousand members by 1928. The group struggled to maintain high standards at the only two remaining black medical schools at Fisk's Meharry Medical School and at Howard. It published a journal, which Kenney edited, and promoted public health. Black doctors therefore administered and staffed their own hospitals, published their own journal, and

promoted their own association. Nurses, dentists, and pharmacists also prac-
ticed in a segregated environment.

Other black professionals faced similar dilemmas during the Jim Crow era.
Lawyers, journalists, teachers, social workers, ministers, and others had to
replicate in some fashion the process of constructing a separate professional
sphere. Paradoxically, segregation encouraged the development of an autonomous black professional class. It also produced the leadership class that later
would overthrow segregation. But segregation meant that black patients, students, and plaintiffs who needed services had to get them from professionals
whose schools and facilities were underfunded, short staffed, and poorly
equipped. As a result, the struggle for control of black professional institutions heightened in the 1920s as the New Negro was less willing to tolerate
these conditions.

The press was another institution that flourished in the African American
community during the 1920s. White-owned newspapers rarely reported on
events in black America and only showed pictures of black people accused
of crimes. Most African American communities had their own weekly papers
that reported on national civil rights news, local politics, social and cultural
events, sports, and the usual local gossip. The newspapers became part of the
community scene, and people were likely to know the name of the editor
and even the reporters. In addition to local newspapers, African Americans
read nationally circulated magazines like the NAACP's *The Crisis*, the Urban
League's *Opportunity*, or A. Philip Randolph and Chandler Owen's *The Messenger*. More popular than these intellectual magazines were the nationally
circulated *Chicago Defender* and *Pittsburgh Courier*. By publishing and reading
newspapers that told African Americans about their own lives, they formed
stable, connected communities. A local newspaper made a place feel like
home.

Because few black-owned newspapers reported to the national circulation
registry, it is difficult to know how many papers they sold. Most were financially stressed. They could pay their reporters very little, and sending one
away on assignment usually required a special fund-raising effort. Revenue
came from advertisers whose products or services were sold to the black community: realtors, insurance companies, clothing stores, restaurants, and the
like. Vendors of personal products like hair tonics and potions for various
ailments did a brisk business, and social groups advertised their events. Sub-
scription fees made up the rest of the income.

Most papers received out-of-town news by exchanging papers with their
colleagues in other cities or by subscribing to the Associated Negro Press

(ANP). Claude Barnett established this service in 1919. A Tuskegee graduate and former writer for the *Chicago Defender*, Barnett paid "stringers" in
many cities who filed stories with the ANP, which he then packaged and
mailed out to his clients. Sometimes such stories would make up most of a
local weekly's content.

The most widely circulated African American paper of the 1920s was the
Chicago Defender. Founded in 1905 by Robert S. Abbott, the *Defender*
appealed to a wide audience by mimicking the sensationalist style of white-
owned mass-circulation tabloids. Abbott ran banner headlines that often
featured sex, crime, and scandal. But Abbott's most important contribution
was to encourage the migration from the South. He printed letters from people planning to leave, train schedules to the North, and advice on what to
do upon arriving in Chicago. Abbott himself was a migrant from South Carolina who saw the exodus as part of the freedom struggle. The *Defender* published both a local and a national edition. The national edition was
circulated by Pullman porters fanning out from the Chicago rail hub, especially on runs through the Deep South. The paper may have sold as many as
two hundred fifty thousand copies per year during its height in the 1920s
and, thus, helped to knit together a national black community.

The *Pittsburgh Courier*, edited by Robert L. Vann, was more intellectual
and less sensationalist than the *Chicago Defender*. Born in North Carolina,
Vann moved to Pittsburgh as a young man, where he continued his education and became a criminal lawyer. Because he was one of only a few African
American attorneys in town, the *Courier* covered his career, and he in turn
began to write for it. By 1926 he had become the editor and owner. Vann
secured a national readership for his newspaper. He assembled an outstanding staff that included George Schuyler, whose barbs skewered white racists,
Garvey supporters, and communists alike. The *Courier* had the best sports
department among the black newspapers. Vann elevated black journalism to
a respectable profession and showed that a national readership could be
found for a sophisticated weekly paper.

While these were the leading black papers of the 1920s, many others
influenced their local communities. Starting on the East Coast, William
Monroe Trotter's *Boston Guardian*, although on the decline by then, was the
voice of his city's emerging South End community. In New York, the *Age*
and the *Amsterdam News* competed for readers in Harlem. Eugene Rhodes
took over the editorship of the *Philadelphia Tribune* in 1921 and led it for the
next fifty years. Carl Murphy edited Baltimore's *Afro-American* for forty years
starting in 1922. In the South, leading newspapers included the *Norfolk Jour-*

nal and Guide and the *Louisiana Weekly*. Among the important Midwestern newspapers were the Kansas City *Call*, edited by Chester A. Franklin, and Wendell Phillips Dabney's Cincinnati *Union*. Most of these papers reflected the views of their publishers. Some featured stories of individual accomplishment and business success, and others were more civil rights oriented, but all helped make each individual black community a unique place. The black press was a key element in making blacks aware of their potential in the 1920s.

By the end of the decade, black America was very different from what it had been at the end of the war. Not only had the population moved, but institutions had grown up to make new neighborhoods into communities. Whether it was a church, school, women's club, or newspaper that made a place feel like home to the people who lived there, the changes of the 1920s made many African Americans feel that part of the country, at least, was their own. While the growth of many of these institutions came in response to changes the Great Migration brought about, the struggle for control of these institutions reflected the new militancy in the black community after World War I.

CHAPTER FOUR

Civil Rights

As African Americans built their own institutions, they also continued the struggle for civil rights. The Northern black communities developed branches of the National Association for the Advancement of Colored People (NAACP), which fought against lynching, disfranchisement, segregation, racism in the criminal-justice system, economic inequality, and colonialism abroad. By 1920, the association had an all-black national leadership and was the leading civil rights group in America. At the same time, rival organizations with different strategies also fought for roughly the same agenda. These groups included William Monroe Trotter's National Equal Rights League and Cyril Briggs's African Blood Brotherhood. During the decade, black voters showed more muscle and independence at the polls, electing several African American state representatives and Oscar de Priest of Chicago to the U.S. Congress. Although the movement for civil rights produced few notable victories during the 1920s, the struggle to rid the nation of legalized discrimination remained at the center of black aspirations. In a thousand local, and a few national, battles, black people showed that they would not stand for Jim Crow laws.

The NAACP had emerged as the leader of this movement by 1919. The association had been founded in 1909 as an alliance of white and black racial liberals. The central black leader before the NAACP was formed was Booker T. Washington, who advocated gradual progress through education, economic advancement, and accommodation to segregation. The NAACP advocated immediate challenges to segregation and political equality. During its first ten years, however, the NAACP had been hampered by internal conflicts and had made little real progress. Its most prominent figure was the founding editor of its monthly magazine, *The Crisis*, W. E. B. DuBois, the only staff member who served on the board of directors. However, DuBois resented white board chairman Oswald Garrison Villard's paternalistic meddling with the magazine's contents. Mediating between them was DuBois's best white friend, Joel Spingarn. Throughout its first decade, the association had a white executive secretary, an integrated office staff, and a small, overwhelmingly African American membership base. Most NAACP leaders felt that the group needed a black executive secretary, but DuBois lacked the leadership skills for that job. The problem was solved after the death of Booker T. Washington in 1915. Several of his supporters joined the NAACP, among them James Weldon Johnson, who became the association's field secretary. In August 1919, Executive Secretary John Shillady was beaten severely by a gang of racists in Austin, Texas, which caused him to resign. The board assigned Johnson to be acting secretary and, in 1920, awarded him the position permanently.

For the first time in American history, black people controlled a well-organized and properly financed civil rights organization. The money came mostly from the overwhelmingly black membership, with some whites contributing larger sums. Its team leadership replaced the pattern of having one charismatic figure represent black people. That role had belonged to Frederick Douglass from the 1840s until his death in 1895 and to Washington for the following twenty years. Johnson, DuBois, and Johnson's assistant Walter White anchored a leadership team that included talented field organizers and local branch activists who played central roles in their communities.

James Weldon Johnson possessed abilities as a writer, speaker, strategist and diplomat that held the organization together. Born in Jacksonville, Florida, Johnson had worked as a lawyer, principal, songwriter, consul in Latin America, and columnist for the *New York Age*. He wrote poems and novels, including *The Autobiography of an Ex-Colored Man*. He had a diplomatic sensibility that the more aloof DuBois lacked, which made him a better organizer.

DuBois edited *The Crisis* throughout the 1920s, winning for it a circulation of one hundred thousand at its peak. Born to a poor single mother in Great Barrington, Massachusetts, DuBois attended the local high school, then Fisk, Harvard, and a German university before returning to Harvard to become the first African American to receive a Ph.D. in history. He taught at Wilberforce University in Ohio and Atlanta University in Georgia, writing historical and sociological studies. In 1903, his thoughtful book of essays, *The Souls of Black Folk*, became a best seller among African Americans and established him as the nation's leading black intellectual. He founded a civil rights organization called the Niagara Movement in 1905, which joined forces with white liberals to launch the NAACP. *The Crisis* became the public face of the association, and DuBois made it into a brilliant, stimulating journal. The 1920s were probably the best years of his professional life because he was not burdened by other duties and could work full time in service to a noble cause.

The last figure in this triumvirate was the youthful Walter White, born in Atlanta in 1893. Johnson brought him to New York, where he had helped lead the branch in a fight for equal education. When White was a teenager, he had helped his father defend their home against a white mob. The aptly named assistant secretary could pass for white, and on several occasions, he risked his life by infiltrating white groups that had perpetrated a lynching. In the New York office, White handled a deluge of correspondence from the branches, vetting complex local problems for the association's still part-time legal committee. Later in the decade, he hosted interracial social events, bringing together writers of the Harlem Renaissance with white colleagues. After Johnson retired in 1929, White served as executive secretary until his death in 1955.

Working with this talented trio was a quartet of field organizers who helped the three to four hundred branches stay in touch with the national office in New York City. The former head of the National Association of Colored Women, Mary B. Talbert, recruited more than a dozen branches in Texas following World War I. Addie Hunton also toured the South, especially in the early 1920s, when many of those branches had to meet secretly to avoid white violence. Both women had served as Young Men's Christian Association workers with African American troops during the war and were widely viewed as angels of mercy by thousands of returning soldiers. Robert Bagnall, a former Detroit minister, worked as national branch secretary throughout the decade. William Pickens, although a Yale graduate and Morgan College dean, had the best "common touch" among all these leaders. As field secretary, he traveled throughout the country to speak on behalf of civil rights and maintain local morale.

Less prominent than these national figures were thousands of branch leaders who confronted authority in their hometowns. While men typically held the key positions and gave the speeches at public functions, women usually did the real work of organizing the finances, conducting the membership drives, and identifying the key issues. Some of these heroines included Alice Nelson Dunbar in Wilmington, Delaware; Lizzie B. Fouse in Lexington, Kentucky; Carrie L. Shepperson in Little Rock, Arkansas; and Olivia Taylor in

Indianapolis, Indiana. Prominent male leaders included Reverend R. R. Williams of Anniston, Alabama; George C. Lucas in New Orleans, Louisiana; Mose Walker in Detroit, Michigan; Butler Nance and N. J. Frederick in Columbia, South, Carolina; and Isidore Martin in Philadelphia, Pennsylvania. These local activists mobilized their communities in times of crisis and held the organization together in slack periods. The civil rights movement of the 1950s and 1960s owed much to the 1920s-era activists.

Some black opponents of the NAACP, most notably Marcus Garvey, charged that the association was white dominated. While there might have been some truth to that assertion prior to 1920, the ascension of the new leadership team proved it false. Although the board of directors remained racially balanced throughout the 1920s, white people on the board functioned mostly as legal advisors, financial contributors, or as conduits to other centers of power. They included Boston attorney and NAACP president Moorfield Storey; Board Chair Mary White Ovington, who encouraged female leaders to step forward within the association; and the brothers Joel and Arthur Spingarn, the latter of whom led the Legal Committee. African American board members typically linked the association to professional groups in religion, law, and medicine, or they led local branches. Debate on the board never divided along racial lines. The leadership came from the all-black paid staff, whose members had long records of service in the black community.

The NAACP fought throughout the decade to outlaw and expose lynching. The Dyer Antilynching Bill did not pass Congress, but it focused public attention on the problem. The association demonstrated in several dramatic cases that law-enforcement officials had colluded with lynch mobs, and they demanded that the perpetrators be prosecuted for murder. Although lynching continued to go unpunished, the efforts of the NAACP helped change the nation's attitude toward mob "justice."

The NAACP chose lynching as a key issue because it so flagrantly offended the American belief in due process of law and because it exposed America to international censure as a violent and racist country. Lynch mobs often did their dirty work in public, and whole towns, including women and children, were encouraged to participate as witnesses. While most of these crimes took place in Southern and border states, some Northern states also saw lynch mobs. Many whites found lynching repulsive, but few did anything about it. They regarded lynching as they did hurricanes or earthquakes—as part of the natural world that could not be changed. The NAACP felt that the war record of black soldiers had shifted national attitudes in favor of outlawing lynching. The association therefore worked with

Missouri congressman Leonidas Dyer, whose district included many black voters, to craft a bill that would make lynching a federal crime.

The reformers challenged contemporary notions of the proper relation between state and local authority. Many people who deplored lynching also believed that it was a local crime over which the federal government had no authority. Prejudiced Southern congressmen, however, hid behind the argument that only the states or local authorities could police criminal acts. After some internal legal debate, the association leaders and Dyer came up with a strong measure. The Dyer bill would allow federal authorities to punish lynchers and local lawmen who colluded with them, even those who stood idly by as blacks were lynched. Counties in which these crimes occurred would be open to civil suits from relatives of the victim. If Congress had passed the bill, it would have contributed in a meaningful fashion to the end of the nefarious practice.

NAACP leader James Weldon Johnson devoted much of his energy in 1921 to lobbying for the bill. The Republican Party, which many contemporaries believed to be the party of Lincoln and friend of African Americans, controlled both chambers of Congress and the presidency. However, there was not one single black representative serving in Congress at the time. Johnson steered the bill through the House Judiciary Committee, answering objections and making some adjustments to the bill's language. Then, the House opened floor debate. Some Southern congressmen openly defended lynching. They argued that it was necessary to protect white women from black rapists, and they used racist epithets in the public debate. Others deplored lynching but argued that there was nothing the federal government could do about it. Black Washingtonians packed the galleries and cheered on the bill's defenders. It passed the House on a party line vote, except for eight Northern Democrats who voted for it.

Johnson continued his campaign in the Senate. Unlike the House, where black voters could influence individual congressmen, no senators felt they had to curry favor with them. Southern Democrats filibustered the bill, tying up all other work in the chamber. The Republicans soon backed down, and the bill never came to the floor for a vote. Neither President Warren G. Harding nor Vice president Calvin Coolidge spoke up for the bill. While both had issued vague statements against lynching, when the time for action came, the Republican leaders capitulated.

Although the bill did not become law, the struggle for it achieved some positive results. The black community and its political leadership developed a new sense of self-confidence. Thousands had acted to change the law by marching and signing petitions. The association bought full-page ads denouncing lynching in major newspapers. In the 1922 election, some NAACP branches campaigned against Republican congressmen who had abstained or voted against the bill. African Americans showed the whole country that they knew how to fight for political goals with modern weapons. White politicians of both parties saw that black voters were becoming a force in the North. Black leaders moved away from pledging their vote in advance to the Republicans.

Aside from lobbying for legislation, antilynching activists also tried to expose these mob crimes. This had been the original tactic of Ida B. Wells. Starting in the 1890s, Wells wrote articles demonstrating that the victims were usually innocent of any crimes, that the perpetrators undermined law and order, and that law-enforcement officials often colluded with mobs. Two dramatic incidents during the 1920s illustrated the horrors of lynching and the efforts of black activists to expose them.

In 1922, a Texas lynching illustrated the depths to which lynchers had sunk. At the town of Kirvin, near Waco, the body of a seventeen-year-old white girl was discovered with multiple stab wounds. The police set bloodhounds on the trail and arrested a black man. Footprints at the scene revealed that three men were present, and the suspect, under torture, named two other black men. A mob burned all three at the stake in the town square, although each swore he was innocent. A subsequent NAACP investigation suggested that the first suspect had been lured to the scene of the crime by two white perpetrators, who smeared him with the girl's blood. Their own motive was rooted in a feud with the victim's family. All three black men, in short, were probably innocent, and the real criminals walked away. Even a racist might be able to see the problem with lynching in this case. If a white perpetrator could always accuse a black man of murder, and the word of a white man always trumped the word of a black man, the result was that no white woman was safe from white criminals.

The NAACP also widely publicized the 1925 South Carolina killing of the three Lowman teenagers. During this incident, an Aiken County sheriff and his deputies, in plain clothes and in unmarked cars, showed up on the Lowman farm, seeking an illegal liquor distillery. Because many lawmen were also Klansmen, they probably knew that the Ku Klux Klan, for obscure reasons, had recently flogged one of the Lowman sons. The sheriff, with drawn pistol, slapped young Bertha Lowman, and her mother, bearing an ax, ran to defend her. The sheriff gunned down the mother, and in response, one of her sons most likely killed the sheriff. The three teenagers at the scene, all wounded and without adequate representation, were quickly tried and found guilty. The judge sentenced the two boys to death and Bertha to life in prison.

The next year a courageous African American attorney from Columbia, South Carolina, named N. J. Frederick appealed the convictions. He hired a white lawyer to assist him. The two men won a directed verdict from the judge to find one youth not guilty. They showed that Bertha was unarmed, and that the only possible shooter was a juvenile. Sensing that some approximation of justice might prevail (in a fair trial all three might reasonably have been found not guilty by reason of self-defense), a white mob abducted all three from jail, with the cooperation of the sheriff. They were transported out of town. The Klan mobilized a thousand people to witness the murder of the three African American youths in a nearby clearing.

The newspapers reported the lynching just as local officials described it. They claimed that a few unknown persons had broken into the jail, overwhelmed the guard, seized the prisoners, run away, and executed them. Unfortunately, the perpetrators could not be found. The NAACP knew this account to be unlikely. Acting on tips from a disgruntled former Klansman, Walter White traveled to Aiken incognito. He discovered nineteen ringleaders, most of whom were connected to local government and the Ku Klux Klan. The *New York World* then sent an investigative reporter, and for the next month, the sheriff's story unraveled on the front page of a leading Northern daily. At last the pressure forced the governor to convene a grand jury, which predictably failed to return an indictment. Most South Carolina newspapers condemned the lynching and the cover-up, signaling a changing attitude among some sectors of the state's elite.

Lynching declined dramatically during the 1920s. Seventy-six African Americans were lynched in 1919; seven were lynched in 1929. While racial violence would flare anew during the 1930s Depression, the late 1920s showed the first real signs of hope. Probably the most important cause for the decline in the number of lynchings in the 1920s was economic in nature. When cotton prices fell, many black people chose to move to the North rather than risk a confrontation with their landlords. Closely connected to this development was the rise of industry in some Southern cities. Northern textile mill owners looking to relocate preferred places in which race relations were stable. Southern elites who wished to encourage new businesses wanted to show that law and order, not unchecked violence, prevailed in their towns.

A probable second cause for the decline of lynching was the revolution in culture and communications. Although much of the rural South was not yet electrified, people could now come into town and see a talking picture show or visit a neighbor with lights and a radio. The whole country enthused over movie actors like Rudolph Valentino or aviators like Charles Lindbergh. Mass entertainment replaced isolated village experience as the center of shared cultural life. Lynching gradually became a throwback to some pre-modern time as a new generation turned its attention to the modern national culture of making money and having fun.

Civil rights activists also played a part. While the Dyer bill did not become law, it did not fail by much. The NAACP's congressional battle put pressure on Southern elites to behave more like Northern elites, who valued law and order. Modernizing Southern leaders put pressure on local bigots not to embarrass their towns or states by creating an ugly incident that might spur a new attempt to pass a national law. Elites were always uncomfortable with mob action anyway. Once violence was deployed against outcast black people, the upper classes worried that it might also be directed against them in an economic uprising.

In addition to lynching, African Americans protested all forms of segregation during the 1920s but met with limited success. They stopped the spread of legally mandated residential segregation but could make no headway against restrictive covenants in real estate transactions. Education remained completely segregated in the South and slightly integrated in the North, although no laws dictated that it exist there. African American activists blocked Northern attempts to mandate educational segregation in the North but showed an ambivalent attitude toward enrolling black children in hostile white schools. The NAACP began its campaign against legal segregation in the South by documenting the disparities between spending on white and black schools.

Activists won some victories in the field of residential segregation. White Americans as a rule preferred to live in all-white neighborhoods, and most did. African Americans probably had mixed feelings about residential integration. Most could not afford the rents in white neighborhoods, and most probably distrusted whites. But few, if any, would grant whites the power to establish racial zoning in housing. Oddly enough, in many Southern cities, the races lived closer together than in the North because so many black women walked to the homes of whites, where they worked as domestics. During the 1920s, white people tried to keep blacks out of "their" neighborhoods by three means: municipal zoning ordinances, restrictive covenants, and violence.

Municipal ordinances mandating residential segregation had a fatal legal flaw: they restricted the rights of white people to sell their property to whomever they pleased. When Louisville, Kentucky, passed such an ordinance, the NAACP successfully challenged it in a 1917 Supreme Court case. The association set up a case in which a black purchaser contracted to buy property in a "white" neighborhood from a sympathetic white realtor. The purchaser then broke the contract, citing the segregation ordinance. The white realtor sued, claiming that the law could not restrict his freedom to sell his own property. The Court agreed.

This decision did not stop other cities from seeking to achieve the same ends by crafting more cleverly worded ordinances. In 1924, New Orleans tried to pass such a rule by including an escape clause that allowed a majority of residents on a particular block to obtain a variance by petition. This measure might allow some whites to sell to black purchasers if their neighbors agreed. Whites wanted the law for two reasons: ideological racists wanted it as a matter of principle, and realtors thought it would help property values. Yet, New Orleans was in part residentially integrated because of its unique French past and the recent migration. Also, more than in other cities, notions of "whiteness" and "blackness" were blurred due to centuries of intermingling.

Black New Orleanians, divided into francophone and anglophone neighborhoods, came together to oppose the law. They raised money, fought a public campaign, and when local and state courts failed, took the case to the Supreme Court and won. The city could not tell white people what to do with their property. Suppose a black purchaser offered a white owner more for a property in a "white" neighborhood? In this matter, market values trumped racist values.

However, if private citizens banded together to achieve the same effect without a special law, the Court refused to intervene. Washington, D.C., had the largest proportion of black residents of any major American city. White homeowners there entered into "restrictive covenants" to keep their neighborhoods lily-white. They pledged to sell their homes only to white people. The district's NAACP chapter employed its leading attorney, James A. Cobb, to block this craftier form of residential segregation. In a case known as *Corrigan v. Buckley*, the association argued before the Supreme Court that the restrictive covenant, while an initiative of private citizens, ultimately asked the government to enforce the contract. In the case before the Court, the covenanters had asked the district to stop the sale of a house to an African American family, and the government had complied. Therefore, the

NAACP argued, the covenant was just as illegal as an ordinance. The Court did not agree, and the number of restrictive covenants increased. The association continued to oppose them, but did not finally succeed until 1948, when the Supreme Court ruled the restrictive covenant unconstitutional in *Shelley v. Kramer.*

Eventually, some African Americans purchased homes in "white" neighborhoods. In the 1920s, these purchasers often faced violence. Detroit had the country's fastest-growing black community in the 1920s and, along with it, a housing shortage. African Americans lived dispersed around the city in different wards. Some middle-class African Americans purchased homes in white neighborhoods, and a rising Ku Klux Klan organized gangs to throw stones at their homes. Several of these homeowners sold out quickly.

Dr. Ossian Sweet and his family, however, were not intimidated and bought a home in a white neighborhood in 1925. Like other black families in white neighborhoods, the Sweets suffered a reign of terror. One night an angry mob threw stones through all of the windows as the police stood by and watched. Then, someone within the house shot into the crowd, killing one man and wounding another. The police finally intervened, arresting all eleven people in the house and charging them with murder. The NAACP hired Clarence Darrow, America's most famous attorney, to defend the family. Darrow argued that "a man's home is his castle" and that any person had the right to repel intruders. After two dramatic trials, the juries could not agree on a verdict, and the prosecution abandoned the case. This was probably the first time in American history that a jury failed to convict black murder defendants when the victim was a white man.

The struggle to end housing segregation became of increasing importance in urban areas as a result of the Great Migration. It was not a successful struggle overall, but it laid the groundwork for future challenges. Moreover, incidents like the Sweet case showed that blacks were less willing to accept second-class accommodation.

The battle over segregated education reflected these same issues. Before the wartime migration, many African American children in the North attended integrated schools, often in immigrant neighborhoods. However, as black communities grew in size, some whites began to object that there were too many black students and that they ought to be segregated. A few Northern districts adopted Southern-style segregation. Black parents often had their own doubts about sending their children to school with hostile whites, but most did not like segregation in the North.

In Springfield, Ohio, the school board voted three to two to segregate the

Fulton School because it had a majority black student body. To promote this idea in the small black community, the school superintendent promised that the new school would hire only black teachers. No African American teachers worked at the integrated schools because almost all whites objected to blacks teaching their children. Three prospective black teachers gathered three hundred signatures favoring the plan. The black community divided when the newly segregated school opened in September. Some leaders called for a boycott, with which three-quarters of the community complied. The integrationists took their case to court and won at the local level. Over the next fifteen years, however, as the black community grew, the school became segregated as a result of changing housing patterns.

A more contentious situation arose when hundreds of white students walked out of Gary, Indiana's Emerson High School in 1927. Eighteen black students had been assigned there after attending a segregated grade school. Gary had a rapidly growing black population because of employment opportunities in the steel mills. The city also boasted a progressive school superintendent with a national reputation for educational leadership. But under considerable pressure, he conceded to white demands that Emerson remain segregated and that a separate black high school be built. The city's school system as a whole was largely segregated because of residential patterns, although the vocational high school and some grade schools were integrated. As in Springfield, black parents resented forced segregation and sued to block the new arrangement. They gathered in mass protest meetings, and the black students protested both segregation and the treatment they received from white students. However, the suit was delayed in court and lost on a technicality. The school board yielded on principle but reassigned the black students on an ostensibly residential, rather than racial, basis. Over time, the community's resistance lost its steam, and African Americans accommodated to segregation. As in Springfield, Ohio, many blacks in Gary felt ambivalent about sending their children to school with hostile whites.

In the South, where the majority of African Americans lived, civil rights activists did not consider demanding school integration. There the struggle focused on improving the quality of underfunded black schools, an issue that the national office of the NAACP recognized as a major civil rights problem. The question was posed more acutely when Congress established the federal Department of Education and began dispersing revenues to the states. The NAACP objected, arguing that the Southern states would discriminate against blacks in the allocation of the funds, which of course they did. The association won a grant from the newly established Garland Fund to study the situation in depth. During the 1920s, *The Crisis* published detailed reports from Southern states showing that white teachers were often paid four times as much as black teachers, and that black class sizes and school facilities were vastly inferior. Georgia, for example, spent ten times more for each white pupil than it spent for each African American pupil. These NAACP reports established the framework for the legal assault on the "separate but equal" doctrine that would culminate in the 1954 *Brown v. Board of Education* decision that declared segregation in public education unconstitutional.

African Americans also challenged routine discrimination in the criminal-justice system during the 1920s. Blacks perpetrated few crimes against whites during those years, and the police were notoriously indifferent to crimes involving black victims. However, black people were often wrongly accused of crimes and were executed disproportionately. They rarely served as policemen, jurors, prosecutors, or judges. A dramatic case from Kentucky illustrates the problems blacks faced when they were accused of crimes.

In 1926, a white Kentucky woman alleged that three black men raped her while she was parked in a lovers' lane with her boyfriend. On the flimsiest of evidence, the police arrested a black man, who, in return for a promise of light punishment, implicated Bunyan Fleming and Nathan Bard. At the trial, neither of the whites identified either man as one of the rapists. Despite the lack of any credible evidence, an all-white jury took fifteen minutes to convict the two men, who were later sentenced to death. During the trial, two courageous journalists exposed the whole procedure in a Louisville African American weekly. In response, the trial judge charged both writers with criminal syndicalism and then with libel when he learned that there no longer was a law against the first alleged offense. Despite protests, Bard and Fleming were hung in one of the country's last public executions. The journalists were convicted and fined. Meanwhile, in a Louisville case, a white man who beat and raped a black woman was convicted and sentenced to a year in prison. The black men were hanged for a crime that probably never occurred, while the white criminal was slapped on the wrist. These three cases showed how race hatred deformed the justice system throughout the era of white supremacy.

Blacks suffered capital punishment disproportionately as compared to whites throughout the 1920s. While the federal government did not keep statistics on crime until 1930, most states did during the 1920s. The statistics for the decade indicate that of 437 executions in Southern states, 315 of the executed, or 72 percent of the total, were African American. In the Southern states, blacks made up 25 percent of the population. Like Bard and Fleming, the likelihood is that more of those executed black people were innocent. Very many were certainly punished more harshly than they should have been. Of those executed, 18 percent were convicted of rape. Of the 122 executed whites, only 7 percent of the total were convicted rapists. Clearly, whites were much less likely to be executed for noncapital crimes.

In only one celebrated case, that of the 1917 Houston mutineers, did African Americans win a measure of mercy, if not justice, from white authority, and that was from the federal government. These black soldiers had been subjected to police brutality when off duty. When one of the soldiers attempted to defuse an incident in which a policeman beat a black woman in the street, the policeman shot at the soldier. False rumors flew around the base that the soldier had been killed. A deranged black sergeant then dispersed the unarmed white military officers and ordered his own men to fall into ranks. The sound of gunshots in the night convinced the soldiers that they were under attack by the police and vigilantes. The sergeant marched about one hundred men, most of them angry and all of them confused, into town. There they killed sixteen whites and seriously wounded eleven others. The sergeant then committed suicide. Afterward, the army executed nineteen black soldiers and sentenced scores of others to lengthy prison terms. The Houston mutiny was probably the worst case of rebellion by American soldiers and the bloodiest assault by blacks against whites since Nat Turner's slave rebellion.

During the 1920s, a wide range of African American activists campaigned for clemency on behalf of the soldiers then imprisoned at Leavenworth, Kansas. Many of the prisoners claimed that they had merely followed the orders of their sergeant. Most believed that they were under armed attack by illegally constituted vigilantes. Many claimed never to have fired a shot. After the war, tens of thousands of people signed petitions seeking clemency for the men. The plight of the Houston soldiers became a key issue for African Americans, who sent delegations to military and civil authorities bearing petitions calling for clemency. After further investigations, sixty-three men had their sentences reduced, and only a few remained in prison by the end of the decade. While blacks were unable to stop most of these injustices in the 1920s, they were active in publicizing them and made it clear that they expected better treatment.

Despite injustices and discrimination among African peoples in the 1920s, Northern African Americans were among the most free. Except for Liberia and Ethiopia, the countries of Africa and its diaspora were colonized

(Haiti was then American occupied). African Americans lived in a country whose founding documents nominally subscribed to the equality of all men, although those sentiments did not always apply to them. By 1920, Northern African Americans were among the few blacks who enjoyed political freedom. A vanguard among them therefore felt obligated to champion the cause of their colonial brothers and sisters in Africa.

To further that cause, W. E. B. DuBois organized four Pan-African congresses during the 1920s. These met in Paris in 1919; London, Paris, and Brussels in 1921; London and Lisbon in 1923; and New York in 1927. While there had been earlier such meetings, the 1920s gatherings were more ambitious in their goals and received better coverage in the European press. Delegates from several African colonies and the Caribbean, as well as African expatriates residing in Europe and the United States, attended the congress. They issued a ringing manifesto to the world demanding an end to colonialism. The declaration cried out against the exploitation of African labor and natural resources and the ignorance and disease that accompanied it. It blasted the colonial powers, except for France, because the francophone delegates were pro-French.

After the 1921 congress, the Haitian delegate presented the Pan-African Manifesto to the League of Nations, which ignored it. The congresses as a whole, however, scored several important successes. First of all, they raised the fundamental issue of justice that no white people of the colonizing nations were willing to discuss. Second, they introduced Pan-African-minded activists from many lands to each other. Third, the congresses gained publicity for the anticolonial cause. The meetings of the 1920s thus laid the groundwork for political independence, which began after World War II with the independence of Ghana in 1956 and concluded with the end of apartheid in South Africa in 1990.

A limited parallel to the Pan-African congresses was the NAACP's protest against the American occupation of Haiti. The United States had taken over that nation in 1915 and administered it through an appointed governor. During the occupation, Haitian nationalists rebelled, and American Marines slaughtered thousands of the poorly armed, barefoot rebels. American banks and realtors took control of Haitian financial institutions and lands. The NAACP campaigned to end the occupation and restore Haiti's independence. This goal was not accomplished until 1934, when President Franklin Delano Roosevelt announced a "Good Neighbor" policy in Latin America and withdrew the troops.

The movement was ahead of its time in the 1920s and was limited by objective circumstances. In the United States, people sometimes confused it with Marcus Garvey's "Back to Africa" slogan, with which it had nothing in common. DuBois wanted to bring international leaders together as a team, while Garvey had himself crowned "Emperor of Africa." Moreover, African Americans were too busy with the daily struggle for survival to pay attention to the plight of colonized people. In addition, the Pan-Africanists were divided among themselves. Two African delegates were pro-French and resisted criticism of France, much to DuBois's consternation. Most importantly, the colonial powers were not about to grant even local autonomy to their colonies, and movements that cannot show progress fade away, no matter how just their cause.

Unable to gain self-governance for Africans abroad, African Americans turned to the issue of voting rights at home. By 1920, almost all Southern African Americans were effectively barred from voting. Southern states accomplished disfranchisement despite the unambiguous words of the Fifteenth Amendment that people could not be denied the vote "on account of race, religion, or condition of previous servitude." Beginning with Mississippi in 1890, the states had passed new ballot qualifications, such as literacy tests, property requirements, or poll taxes, that were ostensibly race neutral but whose real intent was to keep blacks from voting. Moreover, the South had become a one-party region by the 1920s. The insignificant Republicans were composed of African Americans and a few business-oriented whites who barely tolerated them. The only elections that mattered were the Democratic primaries. The few African Americans who could vote would only be voting for sure losers.

Some Southern African Americans who could vote began to consider registering as Democrats. Democratic primaries in some areas were becoming contests between pro– and anti–Ku Klux Klan factions, and black voters reckoned that they had a stake in the outcome of such contests. Texas African Americans had more voting opportunities than other Southern blacks because Texas was a part Southern, part Western state with a democratic frontier tradition. During the early 1920s, the state's Democratic Party divided over the Klan issue. Potential anti-Klan black voters wanted to vote in the Democratic primary. However, a recent Texas law barred blacks from participating in the primary.

In July 1924, an El Paso African American, Dr. Lawrence A. Nixon, tried to vote in the Democratic primary and was denied access because of his race. The Texas law's proponents asserted that the Fifteenth Amendment did not apply to primary elections. Primaries had emerged in the late nineteenth century and were therefore not contemplated by the amendment's framers, they claimed. Nixon and his NAACP attorneys fought through the local courts and won their case on the narrow legal basis that the state conducted the election. Texas next passed a limited law giving county parties, rather than the state government, authority to supervise their primaries. Black voters were shut out again. Some county parties simply barred black people from membership. The NAACP would not finally defeat the white primary until 1944 in a Supreme Court decision known as *Smith v. Allwright*.

African Americans could vote in the North, and especially during the 1920s, many were eager to exercise their right. One reason for heightened voter awareness was the new rise of the Ku Klux Klan. The new Klan paraded on behalf of Protestantism, Americanism, and temperance, but under their hoods, the Klansmen were often racist drunkards. They hated Catholic priests and politicians, Jews making headway in the professions, women who worked, and African Americans who walked Northern streets without showing deference to whites.

The Klansmen aimed to frighten their enemies and also to win political power. In the South and the West, they contended for supremacy in the Democratic Party. At the 1924 Democratic Party convention, Catholics and liberal Northerners sought a condemnation of Klan bigotry. Southern delegates, including Klansmen, watered down the resolution. Since there were few black Democrats, African Americans had little say in this fight. In the North, however, Klansmen dominated several state Republican parties, clamoring for pet issues such as isolationism, Prohibition, and school segregation. Black Republicans therefore called on their party to beat down the hooded bigots within their ranks. Top Republicans, including President Warren G. Harding, who died in office in 1923, and the new president, Calvin Coolidge, deplored the Klan in private but refused to speak out against it in public.

Klansmen achieved their most notable success in Indiana. There a charismatic leader named David C. Stephenson broke with the national organization, which was based in Dallas and too closely associated with pro-Confederate sentiment to make the Klan appealing to Northerners. Stephenson championed American nationalism and disdained the provincial nostalgia for the lost cause of the Confederacy. He celebrated modernity, arriving at his rallies by airplane. The Klan won control of the Republican state political machine in 1924, and Stephenson backed the party's candidate for governor. Black Indianans switched their allegiance to the Democrats. Their slogan became, "Abe Lincoln isn't running this year."

Stephenson's candidate won the election, but power corrupted the Klan leader. While touting temperance and morality in public, he and his cronies organized drunken orgies at his mansion. Then, Stephenson raped a woman, who later committed suicide, and the authorities prosecuted and convicted him. The Indiana Klan went into rapid decline; so did the national movement, just after it staged a 1925 mass march in Washington. In a prosperous time, Americans rejected the violence and extremism that the Klan represented. White Americans may have been racist, but they were not necessarily as anti-Catholic and anti-immigrant, as hypocritical about drinking, or as violently antiblack as the Klan. The Klan was too sectional, and basically too ridiculous, with its hooded robes and cross burnings, to become a serious force. The Klan faded as quickly as it had risen.

The failure of the Republicans to fight for the antilynching bill and confront the Klan made African Americans skeptical of the party's commitment to their cause. Some political leaders drifted toward the Democrats, but most tried to build an independent African American base in the Grand Old Party, from which black people could elect their own leaders. In the 1920 election, African Americans were elected to the state legislatures in New York, West Virginia, Ohio, Pennsylvania, New Jersey, and Missouri. Throughout the decade, more would be elected as legislators and city council members. Using their growing communities as a base, they broke through the typical patron-client relationship that old-fashioned black ward bosses had maintained with urban political machines for years. In the old days, black ward bosses delivered their constituents' votes in exchange for a handful of civil service jobs. The new politicians challenged older conservatives like Perry Howard of Mississippi and Henry "Linc" Johnson of Georgia, who toed the party line in return for a few minor federal appointments for their friends. In Cleveland, for example, independent local politicians, like Harry E. Davis in the state legislature and Clayborne George on the city council, paved the way for the nation's first big-city African American mayor, Carl Stokes, in the 1960s.

The biggest breakthrough, however, came in Chicago. As the city's South Side community grew, its voters elected Oscar de Priest, a veteran community activist, to the U.S. Congress in 1928. For the first time since 1900, an African American would sit in the U.S. House of Representatives. Mrs. De Priest was excluded from the reception given for wives of new congressmen, but her husband became a national spokesman for African Americans. He began as a regular Hoover Republican, favoring conservative economic policies. When the stock market crashed in 1929, he followed the lead of the national party, waiting for market demands to spur recovery. As the Depression deepened, he moved to the left, like most of his constituency, but not quickly enough. After three terms, De Priest lost to an African American Democrat in 1934, signaling a major shift in the black political alignment. Where they could exercise their vote in the 1920s, blacks increasingly attempted to influence elections and gain a political voice.

The NAACP became the nation's central civil rights organization in the 1920s, but some activists remained critical of the group. Some shared the association's goals but had personal disputes with its leaders. They preferred a local leadership, hoping that they could wield more power. Others disagreed with the goal of integrating into American life and asserted that the way to black freedom was to build separate autonomous institutions to meet the community's needs. Still others saw the liberation of black people as linked to the working class, which was conducting its own struggle for liberation.

William Monroe Trotter of Boston exemplified the first type of independent civil rights activist. He founded a local newspaper in 1901 and, later, an organization that challenged Booker T. Washington's conservative leadership. Trotter helped DuBois launch the Niagara Movement, a civil rights group, in 1905, but he quarreled with DuBois over petty organizational matters. When DuBois led the Niagara Movement into the new NAACP in 1909, Trotter refused to follow, in part because he resented having to play a secondary role to DuBois. He teamed up with Ida B. Wells-Barnett in Chicago, a veteran civil rights fighter who also stayed outside the NAACP. A similar figure was Robert L. Vann of the *Pittsburgh Courier*, who resented the NAACP's access to funds from white sources. He accused the association of misappropriating money from the Garland Fund but later retracted his charges. In Detroit, local ministers wanted their own attorneys to get the fees in the Ossian Sweet case, and they tangled with the NAACP over the issue. All four cases illustrate the failure of local leaders to see the value of a necessarily bureaucratic, but therefore more powerful, national organization. None of these leaders articulated a separate national strategy to win civil rights, however.

Other activists offered a more searching critique of the civil rights agenda. Blacks had not been receptive to radical labor or socialism before the 1920s because they faced discrimination from white labor unions and felt obligated to men like Henry Ford, who gave them jobs. However, after the world war, which socialists had opposed as a senseless slaughter, radical labor ideas gained some ground among African Americans. A. Philip Randolph and Chandler Owen in their magazine, *The Messenger*, urged an alliance between black and white workers in the fight against big business. As younger men, they saw civil rights pioneers like DuBois as too conservative. However, DuBois had become increasingly radical as American race relations did not change, and the Russian Revolution seemed more and more like a hopeful beacon to him. DuBois urged black workers and farmers to form cooperative economic associations but warned against class struggle within the community.

The Messenger in the early 1920s attracted several West Indians to its ideas, especially in Harlem. They developed a radical labor and black-nationalist ideology. Some had worked with Marcus Garvey, the most popular black nationalist of his time. Garvey championed black entrepreneurship and investment in his shipping line. The Caribbean-born labor radicals focused on the problems of black workers on the job. They included leaders such as Cyril Briggs, W. A. Domingo, Hubert Harrison, and Claude McKay. Briggs, originally from the Caribbean island of Nevis, published the radical Crusader magazine and organized the African Blood Brotherhood. McKay worked for a while with Max Eastman, editor of a radical magazine, The Masses, and later traveled to Moscow. Domingo and Harrison orated on Harlem street corners, calling attention to the struggles of black workers in the Caribbean. These radical themes would not win a wider audience until the Depression made economic survival a central concern of every working person.

For some, the logical direction of this line of thought led to the Communist Party. This movement was founded in the United States in 1919, two years after the Russian Revolution, and attracted mostly immigrant workers. Unlike their socialist predecessors, the communists took the problem of black rights seriously and tried to recruit black members. With that goal in mind, they launched a front group called the American Negro Labor Congress in 1925. However, the communists burdened their new movement, under orders from Russia, with contradictory notions about joining with white workers while also establishing an autonomous "Black Belt" in the American South. Communists gained few black supporters in the 1920s, but during the Depression, their numbers would swell.

Civil rights activists made no major breakthroughs during the 1920s, but they did begin to turn the tide of triumphant racism. They won significant victories in the Arkansas, white primary, and Ossian Sweet cases. Just as importantly, they built and maintained local NAACP branches that would continue the struggle through the coming decades. Their consistent attempts to challenge injustice and discrimination showed that the New Negro would no longer meekly accept his fate.

CHAPTER FIVE

~

Expressions of Pride

In the Jazz Age, the new black communities of the North gave birth to significant political and cultural movements that affirmed African American pride. Marcus Garvey's Universal Negro Improvement Association (UNIA) put forward a model of separate black identity and solidarity with Africa. The Harlem Renaissance intellectuals and artists crafted characters that maintained a unique identity, yet took their place in American life. African Americans also developed two related musical forms, the blues and jazz, which crossed over into mainstream culture and began to break down racial barriers. Creative artists in all fields, as well as athletes, put forward new role models that undermined racial stereotypes. In a country that blocked black aspirations at every turn, this cultural outpouring showed that African Americans sought to live as proud, free people, despite the intentions of whites.

The most startling and dynamic of these Jazz Age phenomena was the Marcus Garvey movement. Garvey won thousands of admirers by calling on black people to reject white society and build a separate life, an idea that still represents one variant of black nationalism. He argued that African Americans had to focus on their own institutions rather than worrying about their rights as whites defined them. Garvey urged black Americans to redeem colonized Africa and to think of themselves as part of the wider African diaspora, that is, as related to all people of African descent. He championed black entrepreneurship and founded a shipping line that attracted thousands of eager investors. Yet, Garvey proved to be a tragic hero.

Garvey was born in Jamaica in 1887 to a poor family. He had little formal education, having left school for financial reasons. He became a printer and, as a young man, launched his own newspaper, traveling around the Caribbean to report on the conditions of black workers. When his newspaper failed, he departed for London. There he spent two years, mixing with other black expatriates and developing a fascination with Africa. He read Booker T. Washington's autobiography, *Up from Slavery*, and decided to found a school modeled on Tuskegee Institute. Garvey returned to Jamaica and started the UNIA. He planned to visit Washington at Tuskegee, but the school principal died unexpectedly in 1915, and Garvey sailed for Harlem instead.

At first Garvey associated with Harlem radicals like A. Philip Randolph, Cyril Briggs, Hubert Harrison, and others, many of whom were West Indians like himself. But he soon launched an American version of the UNIA. A charismatic orator and bold organizer, Garvey attracted a large following in New York City, especially among West Indians. Garvey electrified his audiences. He told black people to be proud of themselves and that they should cease copying whites and trying to mix socially with them. Blacks, he insisted, should build their own community institutions and businesses. He reminded them that they had traditions and heroes of their own. "Up you mighty race, you may do as you will," he exhorted, striking a responsive chord among people whose aspirations were usually crushed by white people. His preferred term for his people, "Negro," differed from the description "colored people" favored by others. "Negro" implied a distinct ethnicity to Garvey, while "colored people" downplayed the real differences between the races.

Garvey emphasized that American Negroes were an African people. They should think of themselves not as a minority in America, but as part of a mighty international race four hundred million strong. Moreover, he declared that they had a responsibility to help their brothers and sisters in Africa to win national independence. "Africa for Africans" was his slogan. Sometimes he exhorted his followers to go "back to Africa," but this was merely a rhetorical flourish and not a practical program.

Garvey won great popularity by creating the Black Star shipping line. Thousands of contributors bought $5 shares in the company's stock. With their money, Garvey purchased ships that were to carry cargo to the Caribbean and day tourists up the Hudson River. Thousands more paid $1 merely to walk on his first ship when it docked in Harlem. The idea of black people running their own shipping line filled many African Americans with pride and made them want to be part of it. Black people owned, directed, captained, and crewed these vessels.

Finally, Garvey created a sense of optimism among urban blacks who had been disillusioned with the lack of racial progress following World War I. He staged grand parades in Harlem and held mass rallies in New York's largest venue, Madison Square Garden. He appeared before his followers in splendid military outfits, wearing a plumed hat, brocades, and a sword, or in dignified academic robes. At an elaborate ceremony, Garvey appointed himself as provisional president of Africa and assigned its domains to his followers. Garvey established his headquarters at Liberty Hall in Harlem, from which he published the *Negro World*, a newspaper that told of his exploits. In short, he was a master showman for a people longing to see what they could achieve.

Garvey, however, was handicapped by several weaknesses. The most important was that he disdained the fight for civil rights. He had no program for fighting race discrimination; in fact, he conceded that America was a white man's country. He agreed with white segregationists that desegregation would lead to social and sexual intercourse between the races. He thought that white blood degraded the Negro race. In 1922, he met with a Ku Klux Klan leader and declared that the Klan was not antiblack. At a time when lynching went unpunished, some of his supporters began to doubt that Garvey understood what was happening in America.

His African program also ran into problems. He advanced the slogan "Back to Africa," which black people interpreted to mean that they should celebrate their African origins. Garvey hoped to carve out an enclave in Liberia, the only independent state in West Africa. However, the Liberian president feared that Garvey would use his country as a base for attacks against his colonized neighbors, thereby posing a danger to Liberia's independence. Moreover, he did not want to antagonize the United States. Lastly, Liberia's president feared the charismatic Garvey as a rival and thwarted his emissaries.

Garvey's most visible failure was the collapse of the Black Star Line. Neither he nor his associates knew anything about the shipping business. White shipowners sold him antiquated vessels whose boilers quickly broke down. The repair bills piled up more quickly than Garvey could pay them. He canvassed for more investors by implying that his company *owned* two boats that it was merely hoping to purchase. Lastly, when he could not redeem stock certificates for cash, a group of investors claimed that Garvey had defrauded them through the mail. The federal government was happy to charge him and others with conspiracy to commit mail fraud. Although Garvey accused DuBois and his friends of plotting against him, these charges were groundless. Garvey made the further error of representing himself at trial, and he was convicted. Ironically, since Garvey was the only defendant convicted, the charge of conspiracy seemed exaggerated. The likelihood is that many white-owned businesses employed the same unscrupulous practices and never were indicted. Garvey was certainly a bad businessman. The net effect of his enterprise was to coax money from poor black people and give it to double-crossing white men. It remains doubtful, however, that by the standards of the day, his financial crimes merited a term in the penitentiary. He went to prison in 1925.

As his fortunes declined, Garvey and his allies deployed violent tactics against his critics. Around the time of his meeting with the Klan, A. Philip Randolph received a package containing a human hand and a note demanding that he join the "nigger improvement association," a racist reference, probably to Garvey's group. It was signed "KKK." Garvey was not responsible, but instead of denouncing the crime, he accused Randolph of perpetrating it himself. When Randolph and others launched public meetings to denounce him, UNIA members physically attacked them. Then, fistfights turned to murder. On New Year's Day 1923, two Garveyites assassinated Reverend James W. H. Eason, a disillusioned former UNIA leader.

Garvey spent two years in prison until President Calvin Coolidge commuted his sentence in 1927. As an immigrant felon, he was immediately deported to Jamaica. By this time his influence had collapsed, and he was soon forgotten, although the UNIA continued for some years at the local level. His meteoric career paralleled the rise and fall of white businessmen whom everyone admired until the stock market crash of 1929. Before the crash, everyone wanted to emulate the rich. Afterward, they blamed the rich for swindling them. So it was with the flamboyant Marcus Garvey.

Meanwhile, a more influential movement began to emerge in Harlem. This was the artistic flowering known as the Harlem Renaissance. Creative writers and artists in all fields gave expression to the energy bubbling over in the new black communities. For many white writers, World War I had produced disillusionment and despair. While the war did not bring civil rights to America, African American artists nonetheless celebrated the new life they found in the North. They grappled with the legacy of slavery in prose, poetry, and song. Black intellectuals hoped that a literary outpouring would break down the walls of prejudice. In the short term, it did not. However, jazz music gained tremendous popularity in American culture. Writer F. Scott Fitzgerald, author of *The Great Gatsby*, dubbed the era the "Jazz Age." For the first time in American history, an African American cultural product defined a decade.

For the most part, the emergence of a new generation of creative artists was a spontaneous eruption. However, black civil rights leaders soon encouraged the new black artists and writers to flock to Harlem and market their products for the purpose of breaking down racial barriers. Through two journals especially, the National Association for the Advancement of Colored People's (NAACP) *The Crisis* and the Urban League's *Opportunity*, the new writers found their voices, learned to write, and critiqued each other's work.

In a sense, the Harlem Renaissance was wrongly named. There had been nothing like it before in African American history. This was a birth, not a rebirth. The leading Harlem intellectuals understood that they were creating the poems and stories that reflected their escape from Southern Jim Crow laws through the migration. After the civil rights movement of the 1960s, American scholars came to understand that the Harlem writers had contributed significantly to the nation's literature and that the works of Zora Neale Hurston, Langston Hughes, Countee Cullen, and others are central to the American experience.

Editors, poets, authors, and critics all contributed to the ferment. Three editors in particular helped organize the discussion of new questions that the writers all faced. At the Urban League's *Opportunity*, Charles Spurgeon Johnson encouraged black writers by publishing their work and offering cash prizes for outstanding achievements. Johnson, an army veteran who had served in France, returned to Chicago after the war and became research director of the Urban League. After the riot of 1919, he coauthored *The Negro in Chicago: A Study of Race Relations and a Race Riot*, which served as a model for later sociological works. Optimistic, moderate, and a careful strategist, he perceived that changes in race relations would take many decades. Meanwhile, black writers and intellectuals would have to chip away at the stereotypes that whites had erected to marginalize them. As editor of *Opportunity*, he organized a literary awards banquet in 1925. Prominent writers of both races judged the best work of black writers in several categories and awarded prizes. The unprecedented spectacle of interracial collegiality helped to undermine segregation in other professional and social enterprises.

Howard University's Alain Locke probably understood more about contemporary fiction than any other African American writer of his generation. Descended from a prominent Old Philadelphia family, Locke graduated from Harvard with honors, became the first African American Rhodes scholar at Oxford in England, and completed his studies in Paris and Berlin. Returning to America, he became a professor at Howard University and a literary critic. In 1925 *Survey Graphic* magazine asked him to edit a special edition dedicated to the new Harlem writers. Locke expanded it into an extensive anthology later that year. He selected the best black fiction, poetry, drama, and essays about music, folklore, education, and intellectual life. The anthology influenced other writers, and students still read it today.

Jessie Redmon Fauset was unique among the trio because she was the only woman, as well as a novelist and poet. Like Locke she came from an Old Philadelphia family, but hers had fallen on hard times. Nevertheless she graduated from Cornell and secured a job teaching French at Washington, D.C.'s Dunbar High School. W. E. B. DuBois encouraged her to move to New York and edit *The Crisis*'s literary department. Here she encountered one of the important questions that all Harlem Renaissance authors faced: should black writers deliberately create positive images of their people to further the civil rights agenda, or could they also create characters whose behavior was less than admirable? While Fauset opposed the idea of limiting art to propaganda that furthered the black cause, she was committed to writing about educated, dignified people like herself. As editor, Fauset especially promoted female writers such as Gwendolyn Bennett, Nella Larsen, and Dorothy West.

African Americans had a longer tradition in poetry than in any other literary field, dating back to the Revolutionary War–era writings of Phillis Wheatley and continuing through the work of turn-of-the-century poet Paul Laurence Dunbar. The 1920s produced many good poets, but the most prominent were Claude McKay, Countee Cullen, Langston Hughes, and James Weldon Johnson.

McKay immigrated to the United States from Jamaica. After brief stays in Alabama and Kansas, he arrived in New York in 1914. There he associated with an interracial group of Greenwich Village radicals and became coeditor of the *Liberator*. McKay visited England and later the Soviet Union, where he made a speech in the Kremlin and stood on the reviewing stand for a May Day parade. His poems, such as "If We Must Die" and "The White House," reflected the anger and disappointment he felt about American race prejudice. "If We Must Die" celebrates the heroism of blacks who fought back during the attacks of 1919. Although many contemporaries held him in high regard, McKay never quite felt accepted in literary Harlem, and he antagonized its leading editors with his radical politics.

A less political and more popular writer was Countee Cullen. He was an orphan adopted by a leading Harlem minister and NAACP loyalist. Cullen conducted himself with a winsome, politic dignity, befriending many but maintaining a gentlemanly reserve. His poems are less race conscious than those of his contemporaries, quietly mocking prejudice in "Tableau" or celebrating African roots in the often-quoted "Heritage" ("What is Africa to me?" the poet asks in each verse). An air of melancholy pervades some of his poems, whose spare lines capture the joys and sorrows of daily life.

The most popular of all the Harlem writers, and probably the best-known African American poet, was Langston Hughes. Born in Kansas, Hughes's feuding parents moved him between Mexico and the Midwest. He briefly attended Columbia University in New York but dropped out to work at odd jobs and write poems. He shipped out as a merchant seaman for Africa and Europe, broadening his horizons and gaining new material for poems. Despite his difficult childhood, Hughes possessed an amiable disposition. He wrote more poems than his contemporaries and produced several that have become classics. "The Negro Speaks of Rivers," appeared in 1921, a meditation on the African past and its imprint on African American sensibility.

Few people in the arts have been as multitalented as James Weldon Johnson. He is best remembered for *The Autobiography of an Ex-Colored Man* (1912) and *God's Trombones: Seven Negro Sermons in Verse* (1927). During the 1920s, while serving as NAACP secretary, he edited *The Book of American Negro Poetry* and two editions of *The Book of American Negro Spirituals.* In the early years of the decade, he also wrote a sparkling column for the *New York Age.* After leaving the NAACP in 1929, he published *Black Manhattan,* a history of black New Yorkers in the arts. Johnson's literary accomplishments alone would have made him a memorable figure in African American history; that he also led the NAACP at the time makes him a central Jazz Age figure.

The best-remembered collection of Johnson's poems is *God's Trombones.* Johnson wrote it after hearing a preacher who, sensing he was losing his audience, set aside his prepared text and held the congregation spellbound with an oration straight from the heart. The poetic sermons include "The Creation," "The Prodigal Son," and "Go Down Death." In the latter, Sister Caroline faces death bravely because she knows she is going to a better place. The remaining sermons, regarding Noah, the flight from Egypt, the Crucifixion, and Judgment Day, reassure the readers/listeners that their suffering on Earth has a purpose. An African American congregation could understand that "Let My People Go," about the Jewish exodus from Egypt, was about them. Johnson's work later influenced James Baldwin, author of *Go Tell It on the Mountain, The Fire Next Time,* and other works with religious themes.

Of all of the Harlem Renaissance novelists, Zora Neale Hurston is perhaps the most widely read today. She was born in Eatonville, Florida, probably in

1891. At age fourteen, her mother's death caused her to leave school and find work with a traveling theater group. Later, she finished high school, attended Howard University, and graduated with a degree in anthropology from Columbia University. During the 1920s, she studied anthropology, collecting the stories of rural black people in the South. She was a forceful personality on the literary scene and blessed with a devilish tongue. Hurston mocked paternalistic whites who sought undue influence among black writers as "Negrotarians." Her most lasting contributions to literature came in the 1930s, when she wrote *Jonah's Gourd Vine* and *Their Eyes Were Watching God*. She developed morally complex characters whose psychological depth went beyond that of the characters found in the work of more propagandistic, politically minded writers. Her female characters were especially vivid and recognizable. Hurston returned to Florida, and her writing was forgotten. It was rediscovered by scholars in the 1970s and 1980s and has recently enjoyed the attention it deserves.

As a novelist, Jessie Fauset wrote about people like herself: high-minded, dignified people who were comfortable being black and American. Her novels present middle-class, light-skinned, sophisticated, responsible characters who adjust to the difficult realities of American race relations without internalizing the negative stereotypes that whites project upon them. If they seemed a little Victorian to 1920s readers, they also represented something new in American literature: African American characters who defy stereotype and find a measure of happiness. Both Walter White and W. E. B. DuBois wrote similar novels that focused on civil rights and racial injustice in attempts to portray positive images of African Americans.

As civil rights activists, Fauset, White, and DuBois all wrote fiction with an eye toward breaking down stereotypes about black people among educated whites. They realized that unredeemed bigots would not learn anything from them. But many educated whites believed black people to be less responsible than whites and more sensual, artistic, and inclined toward vice. Black people therefore deserved their rural poverty and would not function well in an industrial society that demanded precision work and punctuality. Other whites accepted the same stereotype but saw it as positive: blacks were true to real human nature and therefore happy. Whites had sacrificed happiness on the altar of commerce, and to recover their true selves, they had to learn from black life.

The first novelist to produce an important "race" story in the 1920s, however, had the least connection to the Harlem writers. This was Jean Toomer, whose 1923 novel *Cane* reflected his own ambivalent racial identity. Toomer was born into an elite Washington family; his father was the son of a white planter and his slave. When his biological father left the family and his mother died, Toomer returned to Washington as a teenager. He later became a school principal in Sparta, Georgia. This experience provided the material for *Cane*, which attacked the pretensions of upper-class blacks. The book won an enthusiastic critical response but, not surprisingly, few readers. Despite Toomer's excellence as a writer, his hypocritical characters did not suit DuBois's ideas of good literature.

If DuBois disapproved of Toomer, he was furious with the white writer Carl Van Vechten. When Van Vechten published the 1927 novel *Nigger Heaven*, which dramatized all of the vices of Harlem life, a loud debate ensued among African American writers and critics. DuBois damned the book as salacious trash. Others, mostly younger black writers, were inspired by Van Vechten's flamboyant break from political correctness. Led by editor Wallace Thurman, they published an independent quarterly called *Fire!!* The contributors included sexually explicit writers such as Richard Bruce Nugent and Eric Walrond. Their work showed the full range of human behavior and passion, affirming contemporary values that offended the more conservative (in their literary tastes, at least) civil rights establishment. When *The Crisis* solicited opinions regarding this debate, most creative writers asserted that they would write as they pleased without regard for political niceties.

Were the civil rights literati right to think that African American literature would help to break down racial barriers? In part, they were, especially over the long term. For the country's cultural elite, it did matter that interracial socializing became acceptable. Today, it is easy to forget that the New York writers of the 1920s helped break down the racist taboo against "social equality." Gradually, the possibilities that these writers displayed worked their way into the broader culture. Their most important contribution to American life, however, was the literature itself. The poems and stories caused thousands of readers to understand that their lives mattered, that their problems were common to millions of other black people, and that their hopes might someday be realized. In short, the Harlem writers made African Americans feel proud of themselves. They helped create a sense of identity not just among readers but also among millions of others who did not buy books.

More immediate in its impact and more widespread in its appeal was the music created by African Americans in the 1920s. Black listeners and dancers flocked to juke joints, nightclubs, and dance halls across the country. The music also won white audiences. Serious composers like George Gershwin incorporated jazz styles and instrumentation into symphonic works that became part of the classic American repertory. For the first time in American history, a black-created art form commanded the attention and admiration of millions of whites. Jazz and the blues undercut the habits of segregation much more immediately than did literature.

Jazz was born around the start of the twentieth century in New Orleans. The distinctive product of French-speaking Creoles and African Americans, the music was soon taken up by white players, who brought their own creativity to the bandstand. Jazz combined African rhythms, blues-inflected chord progressions, church spirituals, European melodies, and American marching-band instrumentation. The new sound featured improvisation on a melody line, syncopation, tension between the bass line and the melody that made it "swing," and a soulfulness that lent the music a rich, spiritual dimension. Working in marching bands, funeral processions, bordellos, night clubs, and river boats, innovators Scott Joplin, Buddy Bolden, King Oliver, Jelly Roll Morton, Sidney Bechet, Louis Armstrong, and others created America's greatest indigenous art form.

In the 1920s, trumpeter Louis Armstrong combined a brilliant technique, melodic flair, and engaging stage personality that helped the music "cross over" to find a wider audience. From Chicago, King Oliver sent for "Satchmo," as Armstrong was nicknamed, to join his band, and by 1924 he was a phenomenon among musicians and fans. With wife Lillian Harding on piano, Louis Armstrong and his Hot Five played the big jazz venues nationwide and sold thousands of records for the black-owned Okeh label.

While jazz started in New Orleans, it made its way up the Mississippi by river boat and over to the East Coast by train. Harlem did not dominate the music world the way it did the literary world, but it boasted a swinging nightlife. Pianists made Harlem famous in the jazz world. Two of the very best performers were New York natives James P. Johnson and Thomas "Fats" Waller. Johnson absorbed the music of his day, including ragtime, which was an earlier blend of American folk song, African American banjo tunes, and European piano music popularized by Scott Joplin. Johnson played ragtime in a manner that made the chords "stride" through the tune, and the word came to describe his style. While working at a place in Harlem called the Jungles Casino, he entertained a host of Charleston, South Carolina, migrants, mostly longshoremen and their wives. He wrote a stop-time melody appropriate for their wild style of dancing, and "The Charleston," with its exuberant movement, became the hallmark of a sexually liberated age.

His classic "Carolina Shout" is rooted in the ring shout dance of West Africa preserved by Carolinians.

Johnson passed his technique on to the younger and more flamboyant "Fats" Waller, whose father was a pastor at Abyssinian Baptist. Waller played with brilliant flair and wrote memorable tunes that live in the now-standard jazz repertoire, including "Ain't Misbehavin'," "Honeysuckle Rose," and "I'm Crazy 'Bout My Baby," among others. Johnson and Waller joined other Harlem legends Willie "The Lion" Smith and Eubie Blake in all-night sessions at places like Connie's Inn, Leroy's, or the Rock. They worked with arranger Don Redman, bandleader Fletcher Henderson, and dozens of musicians coming in and out of the city.

While New York became the great center for jazz in the 1920s, every city had its nightclubs, musicians, and fans. Washington, D.C.'s large black middle class produced an artist who defined jazz during his lifetime: Edward Kennedy "Duke" Ellington, the greatest jazz composer ever and one of the great American composers. His musical career began in the capital's black society parties. He had little formal musical training and did not even graduate from high school. Yet, the sophisticated musical style he developed matched the elegance of Washington's black upper class. He wrote beautiful, haunting ballads and swinging jump tunes with the intricacy of symphonic composition. Ellington picked his musicians carefully and wrote tunes that featured their individual style, so that the arrangements perfectly balanced ensemble and solo playing. By the mid-1920s, the band had moved to Harlem, where it reached full flower in the 1930s. No one contributed more than Ellington to the standard jazz repertoire, and his numerous compositions include such classics as "Satin Doll," "Take the A Train," and "Sophisticated Lady."

Later in the 1920s, Kansas City became the regional capital for jazz musicians from Texas to Missouri. It was a "wide open" town for any kind of entertainment, and the city developed a thriving music scene. Saxophone greats Lester Young, Ben Webster, and, in the 1930s, Charlie Parker all worked there. Big bands flourished, including those of Bennie Moten, "Count" Basie, and Jay McShann. Singer Mary Lou Williams got her start as an arranger in Kansas City.

The line between black and white in the arts was easier to cross in music than in literature. Sympathetic white writers might choose to write about African American life, but they would necessarily approach the subject as outsiders. Music is more accessible than literature, so it allows for greater cultural interaction among practitioners. Furthermore, music is a performing art, which ultimately raised the question of whether black and white performers could play together. Throughout the 1920s, a talented group of white teenagers would go to the South Side of Chicago to hear King Oliver and Louis Armstrong. In a few years, they had their own bands: Benny Goodman, Gene Krupa, Dave Tough, Bix Beiderbecke, and Pee Wee Russell helped jazz find a broader audience. But blacks and whites did not play together until the 1930s, when black pianist Teddy Wilson joined Benny Goodman's band in Chicago. By the time of World War II, jazz had become America's music.

One type of jazz, with its own special history, was the unique song form called the blues. This was a product of the Mississippi Delta as surely as jazz came out of New Orleans. The delta musicians lived in an all-black world, and most had to do some form of agricultural labor to support themselves. New Orleans musicians could entertain both white and black crowds, but blues musicians sang or played only to poor black folk like themselves. They gathered in rural juke joints or in sharecroppers' quarters on plantations. The area around Cleveland, and Clarksdale, Mississippi, produced an extraordinary number of players, and their music revolutionized American culture in the 1950s when a new generation created rock 'n' roll.

The phrase "the blues" already meant "sorrow" in American slang, but the music called "the blues" could express any emotion. The lyrics state a problem, often about failed love, traveling, crime and punishment, escape, or dreary work, develop it, and resolve it in the course of a chorus or over the whole song. The harmonic roots, some critics think, lie in Africa, but it was invented in America by Americans singing about their own lives. The work song and the gospel song both helped make the blues. Unlike the urban jazz players, blues musicians did not have access to many instruments. They could usually only get a guitar, a near relative to the banjo, an African instrument that slaves recreated in America. So, the blues began with one performer singing and accompanying himself on guitar, tapping out a steady beat with his foot.

Nobody knows just how far back the blues form goes, but the first time a trained musician heard someone playing it was in 1902. W. C. Handy, "Father of the Blues," noticed a black man singing at a delta train station. Handy stayed in Mississippi another two years to learn more. By the 1920s, several delta singers had transformed the blues into an art. They included Son House, Sonny Boy Williamson, and guitar wizard Robert Johnson, who, legend had it, sold his soul to the devil at "The Crossroads" in return for musical skill.

In time, blues singers became more sophisticated and performed with backup bands. The blues provided opportunities for women as well as men, especially in nightclub acts. Mamie Smith had the first hit recording, called "Crazy Blues," which sold seventy-five thousand copies in a single month. "Ma" Rainey of Columbus, Georgia, was another of the great early blues singers. She signed the fourteen-year-old Bessie Smith (no relation to Mamie) to her Rabbit Foot Minstrels, and within a few years, a star was born. Bessie Smith had all of the qualities as a vocalist that Armstrong had on trumpet: a big, expressive sound, skillful musicianship, an expansive range, and a charismatic presence that captivated audiences and sold records. Bessie personified the blues for her listeners: she had fame, money, and an abusive husband, and she suffered a tragic end in a Mississippi automobile accident.

The blues and jazz were mainly new developments, but an older musical tradition continued throughout the 1920s. Negro spirituals, as they were then known, came from the same sources as the newer music, but they were rooted in religious feeling. Probably the best-known choral touring group was the Fisk Jubilee Singers. The leading individual singers, composers, and arrangers of spirituals in the 1920s included Harry Burleigh, Nathaniel Dett, Carl Diton, and David Guion.

African American musical achievement also flourished in the area of classical music. In this field, performers had to confront white upper-class racism in all its arrogance. Roland Hayes was born in1887 to a tenant farmer and his wife, both former slaves, in rural Georgia. Blessed with a magnificent voice, he studied music at Fisk University, toured with its famed Jubilee Singers, and moved to Boston to continue his studies. In 1917, he debuted with the Boston Symphony Orchestra, becoming the first African American to appear with a major orchestra. He toured Europe and returned to America in 1923 after winning over openly hostile audiences in Vienna and other European capitals. He was awarded the NAACP's Spingarn Medal for outstanding achievement in any field in 1924. In composition, William Grant Still introduced African American musical themes into symphonic settings. While many European-oriented musicians were deaf to this innovation, others recognized that "classical" music drew its inspiration from these very same sources.

Until the 1920s, success in music was measured by the number of people who attended performances and by how many copies of sheet music people bought. After World War I, the phonograph became a popular consumer item. More people had electricity in their homes and could afford to purchase this new device. Black entrepreneurs were quick to enter this new field. The most important venture by African Americans in the new recording industry was the Black Swan label founded by Harry H. Pace. Pace came to

New York from Atlanta in 1920 to publish sheet music with W. C. Handy, the composer of "St. Louis Blues." The two men disagreed over business policy, and Pace next turned to recording. He booked blues singers Ethel Waters and Alberta Hunter, but just as their music was starting to catch on, Pace shifted toward classical music. Black Swan's board of directors included several high-art enthusiasts like W. E. B. DuBois, who wanted to emphasize the achievements of classical singers like Roland Hayes and Marian Anderson. Meanwhile, white-owned companies began to record jazz musicians and blues singers, cutting into the market. Pace failed to sign the great blues singer Bessie Smith, who was too earthy for his taste. The company folded in 1924, a casualty of its white competition and its own failure to adapt to market trends.

Jazz and the blues captured the nation's ear. The music let white America hear what black Americans were saying. This cultural exchange flourished in the Jazz Age, and it contributed to the collapse of legal segregation in the 1950s, when young people danced to the music of Chuck Berry and Elvis Presley without caring about either singer's race.

African American creativity flourished in all of the arts during the Jazz Age. Black artists painted, made movies, transformed the Broadway musical, and created serious dramatic roles. They won large audiences of blacks and whites, and for the first time, white dramatists incorporated African American themes into their works.

Aaron Douglas was the leading visual artist of the Harlem Renaissance. Born in Topeka, Kansas, he came to New York as a young man and quickly established an imposing reputation. His drawings combined a spare, modernist style with West African influences. His work graced the pages of *The Crisis, Opportunity,* and such literary works as James Weldon Johnson's *God's Trombones* and Alain Locke's definitive anthology, *The New Negro.* Douglas won numerous awards and earned the recognition of modernist critics. Later in his career, he painted murals at Fisk University and the Harlem branch of the New York Public Library.

The most exciting new art form of the day was the cinema, which added the dimension of sound during the 1920s. Black audiences were numerous enough by the 1920s that theater owners began locating venues in the new black communities. There they could see films by Oscar Micheaux, a pioneer African American producer. He brought to his art a varied life experience: work as a Pullman porter, South Dakota farmer, and novelist. In 1918, he turned his third novel into a film, *The Homesteader,* which he distributed himself, sometimes personally convincing white theater owners to show his movies. Ultimately, he made almost fifty films, which took on such contro-versial subjects as lynching, passing for white, and fraud among African American ministers. Micheaux had to work under very tight budget con-straints, and he barely eked out an existence as an independent producer. Yet, he hired the best actors, including Lorenzo Tucker and Paul Robeson, who became celebrities in the black community during the 1920s. All his films were silent until 1931, when he made the first African American talk-ing film, *The Exile*. Only twelve of the movies still exist; unfortunately, the others have disappeared. Micheaux continued making films until his death in 1951.

African Americans had long contributed to popular culture in vaudeville, a blend of comedy, song, dance, and theater. For decades, New York espe-cially had featured musical artists such as Bob Cole and J. Rosamond John-son, as well as comedians Bert Williams and George Walker. By the 1920s, these traditions came together in hit musicals that captivated black and white audiences. Florence Mills's stage career made her the most famous black celebrity of the 1920s, as she starred in the leading African American musicals of the Jazz Age.

Florence Mills began as a child entertainer in her native Washington, D.C. Later, she played vaudeville houses with her siblings as part of the Mills Sisters. She had a winning personality and, on stage, showed herself to be talented, classy, and at once risqué, virtuous, and vulnerable. Men loved her, and women admired her. Her big break came with the wildly successful hit *Shuffle Along*, written and produced by the team of F. E. Miller, Aubrey Lyles, Eubie Blake, and Noble Sissle. After a short tour to African American ven-ues in Washington, D.C., and Philadelphia, the show opened with uncertain expectations before racially mixed audiences in New York. *Shuffle Along* delivered catchy tunes, including hits such as "I'm Just Wild about Harry" and "Love Will Find a Way," and the most energetic choreography anyone had ever seen. The show brought in record numbers of patrons for a year in New York and another two on the road. Similar shows followed. The song-writing quartet broke up into two pairs, and Miller and Lyles staged the next hit, *Runnin' Wild*. This one introduced "The Charleston" to a wide Ameri-can audience. There would be new shows too, such as *Chocolate Dandies*, which featured Josephine Baker, who would later entertain on the Paris stage.

Florence Mills's last role was in a revue called *Blackbirds*, in which her song "I'm a Little Blackbird Looking for a Bluebird" stopped the show for applause. But at the height of her popularity, Mills died suddenly of appendicitis in November 1927 at the age of thirty-two. Harlem and all of black America was stunned. One hundred thousand people thronged to her funeral procession, at which a flock of blackbirds was dramatically released from an airplane. Florence Mills's untimely death drained the Harlem arts movement of its optimism and innocence.

Just as Florence Mills lit up the musical stage during the 1920s, so did the actor Paul Robeson transform the serious drama. He followed in the footsteps of stage pioneer Charles Gilpin. Both starred in roles created by Eugene O'Neill, the Irish American writer who crafted brooding plays about humanity's capacity for evil and self-destruction. O'Neill had already scripted two plays with African American characters before writing his classic *The Emperor Jones* in 1920. It was first staged in Provincetown, Massachusetts, and starred Gilpin. The central character is a Pullman porter who is shipwrecked in Africa and becomes the local ruler. The play established Gilpin's career, and Robeson further defined the character when the play was staged again on Broadway in 1925.

Paul Robeson played the male lead in O'Neill's next play, *All God's Chillun Got Wings*. This controversial play, which featured an interracial couple, shocked 1920s sensibilities. Only twenty-six when the play opened in 1924, Robeson had already enjoyed a spectacular career as a scholar-athlete at Rutgers University. On the football field, he had to overcome racism from white players who taunted and gouged him in the pileups. After college, he became a lawyer, but disgusted by the very low glass ceiling imposed upon black attorneys, he followed his growing passion for the theater. Robeson had a magnificent baritone voice and appeared next in the musical *Porgy and Bess*. In a separate career as a singer, he performed spirituals and folk songs of many lands. Later, he starred in Shakespeare's *Othello*. After the 1920s, Robeson fought for social justice, singing for Spanish Republican troops during the 1930s and campaigning for civil rights in America after World War II. His career was cut short by the anticommunist witch hunts of that time, and Robeson, who had been enormously popular, became a forgotten figure.

Despite the black artistic triumphs of the time, most white intellectuals of the 1920s believed in the permanent, genetic inferiority of black people. This was the heyday of racist polemics by Madison Grant, Lothrop Stoddard, and others. Their books argued that "Anglo Saxons" or "Nordics" were responsible for the advance of civilization. Therefore, they postulated, intermarriage should be banned, and black Americans should be kept as second-class citizens. In the field of American history, Southern apologists for slavery argued that Reconstruction had been an experiment doomed to failure by the inherent inferiority of Negroes. At Ivy League universities, William A. Dunning and his followers published a series of books allegedly showing that black politicians had abused the South and acted in a corrupt fashion during their brief tenure in office after the Civil War.

African American intellectuals rejected this line of argument virtually by themselves, save for such white scholars as Franz Boas in anthropology and Melville Herskovitz in history. DuBois published articles in *The Crisis* that skewered these claims. Educators Herbert Adolphus Miller, Horace Mann Bond, and others showed that racist educational psychologists, relying simply on test scores, failed to account for the miserable education afforded black children in the South. DuBois himself debated Stoddard in a dramatic 1929 confrontation before a packed auditorium in Chicago. During the 1930s, DuBois would publish his classic work on Reconstruction that refuted the Dunning school, which is now entirely discredited.

For DuBois, the 1920s were fruitful years for editorial work and essay writing. In *The Crisis* he published articles on politics, literature, international events, economics, and other matters not necessarily related solely to African Americans. During this time, DuBois traveled to the Soviet Union, drawing a favorable, if naïve impression of the communist revolution, although he doubted it would work in America. He published articles by radical economist Abram Harris and championed cooperative economic endeavors by producers and consumers.

While DuBois was the most visible black intellectual of his day, others whose long careers spanned the 1920s made valuable contributions during that decade. Carter G. Woodson launched Black History Week in 1926. The Virginia-born educator had earlier launched *The Journal of Negro History* and the Association for the Study of Negro Life and History, which by the 1920s were attracting a new generation of black scholars. As a historian, Woodson wrote three books and edited several others during the 1920s. He focused on social and economic history, regarding the lives of ordinary people as central to his research.

Sociologist Edward Franklin Frazier represented the next generation of black social scientists. Educated at Howard, Clark, and the University of Chicago, Frazier directed Atlanta University's School of Social Work from 1922 to 1927. When he published a blistering attack on race prejudice in a respected magazine, enraged Atlanta whites drove him from the faculty. His research focused on the family and social class relations. A 1925 essay on the black business class served as the basis for his controversial criticism of middle-class political timidity in *Black Bourgeoisie*.

While black scholars exercised their intellectual abilities, black athletes earned respect for their physical abilities. Blacks had been playing baseball almost as long as whites, and before the sport became segregated, black players established a foothold in the early white baseball leagues. Among the best players of the nineteenth century were black infielder John "Bud" Fowler, who was born, suitably enough, in baseball's birthplace of Cooperstown, New York; Moses "Fleetwood" Walker; and Ulysses S. Grant, who batted 0.340 for the Buffalo Bisons in 1886. But the curtain came down on interracial baseball in 1887 when Adrian "Cap" Anson, a fire-breathing racist, refused to play against Walker and pitcher George Stovey. The baseball league endorsed Anson's boycott, and blacks henceforth played on separate teams.

These all-black teams led a haphazard existence. Professional and semipro teams came and went, struggling to maintain schedules and keep financial structures intact. By the 1920s, three separate black leagues existed. The strongest franchises in the Midwest were in Chicago, Detroit, St. Louis, Indianapolis, and Kansas City. The Eastern Colored League boasted teams in Manhattan, Brooklyn, Philadelphia, Atlantic City, Baltimore, and Harrisburg, Pennsylvania. Southern League teams played in several cities, but the Birmingham Black Barons, who had a star pitcher named "Satchel" Paige, were the best.

The baseball teams became a source of pride for the whole community. The Kansas City Monarchs won the first Negro League championship in 1924 behind the pitching of "Bullet" Joe Rogan. On Sundays, five thousand fans, dressed in their best outfits, attended the games. Businessmen formed booster clubs to back the teams, and the players were hailed as local heroes. The Monarchs even had white fans. Detroit African Americans cheered for Norman "Turkey" Stearnes and the Detroit Stars. The Negro League at first did not keep accurate statistics, but many observers argue that Stearnes was the leading home run hitter in history. As record keeping became more standardized, Stearnes frequently led the league in home runs.

Fans who could not attend the games could follow the action in the black press. The Indianapolis Freeman covered the game better than any of its rivals. Their local team had perhaps the best player in the game in 1921, Oscar Charleston. In the Eastern League, the Philadelphia Tribune gave extensive coverage to its team, the Hilldales. The Chicago Defender covered several local teams, and the Pittsburgh Courier kept fans up to date on the Homestead Greys. Both built their national circulations in part on their baseball coverage. Black athletes were a source of pride for all African Americans, and sports provided another, albeit segregated, arena to showcase the race's capabilities.

In the short term, the influence of Marcus Garvey, the Harlem writers, the musicians, the intellectuals, and the athletes proved limited. In the 1930s, the onset of massive unemployment and serious poverty for millions of Americans, especially African Americans, pushed the concerns of the Roaring Twenties to the side. The mood changed from exuberant to somber, determined, or desperate.

Yet, no meaningful cultural creation disappears forever. The legacy of the Harlem writers was revived with the interest in black history during the 1960s and afterward. A new generation of African American writers took center stage in American literature in the last half of the twentieth century. These included Ralph Ellison, Toni Morrison, James Baldwin, and Alice Walker, whose books found millions of new readers and were sometimes made into films. A new generation of scholars rediscovered the writers of the 1920s, and many of their works were reissued.

Garvey's theme of black pride was reinvigorated in the 1960s, and figures such as Malcolm X and Stokely Carmichael (Sekou Toure) called for "Black Power." Jazz musicians reemerged, reinventing the music as bebop, an intense style that demanded serious listener attention. Black athletes broke down the barriers to participation in American sports and became heroes to white fans. Intellectuals rewrote American history so that the national understanding of our entire past has been transformed. These profound changes in American life all had their roots in the Jazz Age.

Epilogue

In the spring of 1927, a flood of epic proportions spilled over the lower Mississippi Delta. The mighty river's waters killed over five hundred people, left half a million homeless, and wreaked over $1 billion in damages. Most of the victims were African American sharecroppers and tenants. What little they had was lost.

The survivors streamed into Red Cross refugee camps, but the federal government refused to declare an emergency. African Americans all over the country sent money and clothing, and the disaster brought out the best among some white Southerners, who also pitched in to help. But white Southerners above all wanted to maintain control of "their" sharecroppers. Black people were confined in the camps, often against their wishes, by armed guards. Young men were put to work, sometimes at gunpoint, and forced to rebuild the levees. White refugees were spared these indignities. Though no one could see it at the time, this enormous disaster foreshadowed an economic catastrophe that lay ahead.

Times were already hard for black people by the late 1920s as the economy began to slow down. Slow economic growth was caused by a combination of overproduction and the uneven distribution of wealth that limited how much poor people could buy. As businesses cut back on production, African American workers lost their jobs more rapidly than whites lost theirs.

When the stock market collapsed in October 1929, business confidence declined. Capitalists cut back production still more, factories closed their doors, depositors rushed to banks to withdraw their savings, and the banks went out of business, ruining millions. The numbers of jobless grew, and men hit the road as hoboes, looking for work, clustering in shanties known as

"Hoovervilles" for President Herbert Hoover. Black unemployment rates were three to four times higher than those of whites. For many, only a tiny relief check and a charity soup kitchen kept starvation at bay. Hunger became a real problem as crops rotted in the fields for lack of buyers. The migration north trickled to a halt, for there were no more jobs. In an unusual display of interracial cooperation, white and black veterans marched on Washington, D.C., to demand early payment of the bonus guaranteed them for wartime service. The army broke up the march, but the reduced racial antagonism suggested new possibilities.

Familiar patterns, however, reemerged. In the early days of the Depression, some whites turned their anger, as they had done before, on black people. Lynching statistics, which had declined to the single digits by the late 1920s, rose perceptibly. In 1931, two young white women accused a group of black youths of raping them, and the celebrated Scottsboro, Alabama, case began.

In 1932, the voters elected Franklin D. Roosevelt as president. A hesitant upturn in the economy gave workers renewed confidence, and a wave of strikes broke out in 1934. As the Roosevelt administration liberalized the labor laws, the Congress of Industrial Organizations began organizing basic industry, and white workers gradually started to accept black members in the new unions. Class antagonisms replaced the usual racial solidarity of white workers. Roosevelt's New Deal created new government jobs, and most African Americans cheered his proposals. But the president was reluctant to challenge powerful Southern Democrats in Congress, who chaired many important committees. The New Deal excluded tenant farmers, sharecroppers, and domestics from the new programs. Administrators excluded African Americans from jobs in the Civilian Conservation Corps (CCC) and the Tennessee Valley Authority. The New Deal, at first, was for whites only.

African Americans fought back through institutions that had been strengthened or established during the 1920s. The NAACP, Urban League, church leaders, and others insisted that the administration change its policies. Gradually, it did. First Lady Eleanor Roosevelt was openly sympathetic to black demands for equal treatment by the federal government, and she arranged for meetings between the president and black leaders. Over the next few years, Walter White, Mary McLeod Bethune, A. Philip Randolph, and others made their voices heard in Washington. Eventually, about three hundred fifty thousand black men found work through the CCC, and thousands got jobs in other relief agencies. Thanks to the New Deal labor legislation, the Brotherhood of Sleeping Car Porters won its battle with the Pullman Company for union recognition. In 1941, when defense plants refused to hire black workers, Randolph threatened Roosevelt with a march on Washington, and Roosevelt agreed to create the Equal Employment Opportunities Commission. The 1941 movement presaged the 1963 March on Washington for Jobs and Freedom.

The New Negro of the 1920s thus contributed to the progress of later generations. The migration, checked in the 1930s, increased in tempo after World War II. Institutions that developed in the 1920s, from the NAACP to the churches, flourished later as well. The pride and self-assertion championed by Marcus Garvey found new expressions in the post–World War II freedom movement. Black writers and musicians deeply affected American culture in the 1950s and 1960s, challenging racist assumptions and breaking down old taboos. The New Negro of the 1920s, by forging a decade of struggle and promise, made possible the gains of forty years later.

Documents

Chapter 1: Black Hopes, White Fears, Red Summer

There had been race riots in the United States prior to the summer of 1919.The most notorious examples took place in New York City in 1863, Atlanta in 1906, and East St. Louis, Illinois, in 1917. Fueled by false rumors and economic insecurity, white mobs attacked black communities, looting, burning, and killing with impunity. The best defense for African Americans was to get off the street, but many were not safe even in their own homes. Military service in World War I changed the attitudes of young African Americans when a wave of racist violence broke out after the war. Blacks began to fight back.

The African American press hailed the new mood as a positive development. The Baltimore *Afro-American* (document a) welcomed the restraint of black citizens and their "preparedness," to borrow a term from the prewar debate about the nation's military. Its front-page cartoon showed the Capitol building literally in the grip of a white thug. The *Washington Bee* (document b) noted that white servicemen "started it" and that the police enforced the law only against black people. In general, the African American press welcomed the appearance of a "New Negro."

By contrast, the *New York Times* (documents c & d) blamed the violence on radical agitators. The paper covered the events on its front page, reporting on a New York meeting of African Americans. The audience had come to hear a speech by William Monroe Trotter regarding his plea before the Paris Peace Conference on behalf of African Americans, and at that meeting they cheered Washington blacks for their resistance to white attackers. Yet, the editorial, without any evidence, blames white radicals for stirring up trouble.

Walter White was uniquely placed to write longer postmortems on the riots. As a teenager, he had defended his own home, crouched next to his father with a gun in his hand, during the 1906 Atlanta riot. He could "pass" for white, and as an adult, he investigated several lynchings by pretending to be sympathetic to the lynchers. As assistant secretary of the National Association for the Advancement of Colored People (NAACP), he reported on the Chicago riot for *The Crisis* in the article reprinted here (document e). His article serves a different purpose. White analyzes the events like a social scientist, showing that the spontaneous violence was rooted in deeper social problems.

The 1920 letter from S. H. Tarbet to the NAACP sheds light on the origin of the Elaine, Arkansas, massacre (document f). Tarbet's information is third hand, but it might be the best explanation for the start of the Arkansas riot. According to Tarbet, a gang of whites attacked a meeting of black sharecroppers. When two white men and a black driver stumbled onto the scene, the white gang shot at them also. Later, twelve black men were wrongly convicted of murder for the deaths of these white men and others. The NAACP ultimately won their freedom after a long legal struggle.

Lynching did continue, albeit at a lesser rate. Two stories, one in the white-owned *Vicksburg Herald* (document g) and another in the African American *New York Age* (document h), show contrasting views of the same event.

Sources
"Washington Riot," *Afro-American* (Baltimore), July 25, 1919.
"They Started It," *Washington Bee*, July 26, 1919.
"Urge Negroes to Use Force to Get Rights," *New York Times*, July 28, 1919.
"Race Riots," *New York Times*, July 28, 1919.
Walter White, "Chicago and Its Eight Reasons," *The Crisis*, April 1920.
S. H. Tarbet, letter to NAACP from Arthur Waskow Collection, Wisconsin State Archives.
"Negro Intruder Lynched," *Vicksburg Herald*, May 15, 1919, and *New York Age*, June 14, 1919.
"Negro Was Lynched to Save White Woman's Secret Lover," *New York Age*, June 14, 1919.

a. "Washington Riot," *Afro-American* (Baltimore), July 25, 1919
The only thing that kept the Washington riots from causing as severe a loss of life as the East St. Louis massacre was the *preparedness* of Washington's

colored population. Not in all cases, but in a fair proportion, armed colored men and women used revolvers to good effect on the mobs attacking their homes. The result has been that white marines, soldiers and sailors inciting the outbreak confined their attentions largely to single individuals thought to be unarmed and without hope of early assistance.

Inability of the Washington police to locate the maniac, who has assaulted one colored and several white women, is given as the cause of the riot. Whites agreed, began to hold the whole colored population responsible for the assaults, and attacked innocent Negroes wherever they could be found.

One of the lamentable features of the affair was that in practically every instance, white sailors, soldiers or marines were foremost in the fighting. With disgraceful disregard for the obligations which go with the wearing of the uniform, these men took the lead in fomenting riots and assaults relying on their familiarity with firearms to cow the Negroes.

To the credit of the colored citizenry in the capital, it can be said that in the first stages of the riot no single colored man took the initiative in creating disturbances. Every time whites were the aggressors, until human nature could stand it no longer, and in pure defense groups of men in fifties and hundreds went out to show the attackers that the colored population was not altogether defenseless.

One of the results of the rioting will be the bringing home to President Wilson of the disgrace and the extent of mob reign in the country, and the necessity of a firm Federal hand in nipping it in the bud as well as in punishing the offenders. President Wilson's proclamation has had as much effect on mob violence in the country as water on a duck's back. With rioters at the very door of the White House the president must see, unless it is impossible to get his thoughts home from Europe, that sterner measures are necessary.

b. "They Started It," *Washington Bee*, July 26, 1919

The soldiers and marines started the riot against the colored citizens for no cause whatever. It is so strange that every effort was made to disarm defenseless colored citizens and no effort made to disarm the whites. Men were arrested for carrying concealed weapons because they had weapons in their houses—that is, colored men. Detective J. T. Jackson was shot by a white man in the presence of his carpenter, *The Bee* is informed. Was any attempt made to arrest the assailant? Has the city gone wild over the assault made upon a young colored girl, referred to elsewhere in *The Bee*? Why were all colored men arrested and no white men—men who were invading the homes of colored citizens and pursuing them wherever seen? Why were street cars invaded by white men and colored citizens snatched from the cars and no arrests made? But you can see the number of colored citizens tried was convicted in the courts. The police department could not protect the colored citizens so they were forced to protect themselves.

Why did white officers seek colored citizens, disarm them and place them under arrest? It is charged that the bad element of the colored people were in the mob. This *The Bee* denies. The cause of all the colored people was common, and the mob did not respect any colored man or woman, so long as his or her face was black. The authorities were warned and appealed to to give the colored people protection. Monday night representative colored delegations called upon the commissioners and asked for protection, but no encouragement was given them. The commissioners were informed that the colored citizens would do no more than protect themselves. . . .

The Bee extends its gratitude to those white citizens who had the courage and heart to protect the colored citizens to the best of their ability. . . . *The Bee* regrets the death of Detective Wilson. He can only blame himself. At the corner of seventh and Florida avenue, the evening of the riot, he was vindictive toward the colored people. Did he have the right to invade the home of the person who shot him? Did he see a felony committed? Did he witness a murderous assault? If he did, he was justified in entering and his assailant should be punished; if not, he had not the right to enter the home.

No respectable colored person was safe upon the streets. The whites started it, and *The Bee* regrets it. All honor to the white citizens who sided with the law-abiding colored citizens!

c. "Urge Negroes to Use Force to Get Rights," *New York Times*, July 28, 1919, p. 4

Openly taking their cue from the recent uprising of blacks in Washington, nearly 2,000 negroes, meeting yesterday afternoon in the Palace Casino, Madison Ave. and 135th Street, wildly applauded and shouted approval when various speakers appealed to them to "follow the constructive work the blacks did in Washington," and "fight like h—, every one."

Some of the advice the speakers gave the audience was:

"Use all methods to obtain your rights, even force."

"Don't demand your rights—take them."

"Make radicalism the very essence of our propaganda."

d. "Race Riots," *New York Times*, July 28, 1919, p. 10

The outbreak of race riots in Chicago, following so closely on those reported from Washington, shows clearly enough that the thing is not sporadic. . . . [I]t is time for the authorities to stop wool-gathering and begin to find out the facts.

In THE TIMES this morning is printed some evidence which goes far toward suggesting that the Bolshevist agitation has been extended among the Negroes, especially those in the South, and that it is bearing its natural and inevitable fruits. It is rather hard to believe that in such widely separated cities as Washington and Chicago there could be an outbreak of violent racial animosity within a certain number of days, and all without influence or suggestions from any outside source. There is no use in shutting our eyes to facts, and we know that in the early days of the war there was a pro-German and pacifist propaganda among the Negroes, which may well have turned into a Bolshevist or at least socialist propaganda since. . . .

How far the original German propaganda among the negroes may have been utilized subsequently by the I.W.W. (Industrial Workers of the World) we do not yet know. It is apparent however, that there is more in it than occasional flamings-out of race hatred in cities the least likely to harbor such feelings. In other words, the situation presupposes intelligent direction and management.

e. Chicago and Its Eight Reasons, by Walter F. White

Many causes have been assigned for the three days of race rioting, from July 27 to 30 in Chicago, each touching some particular phase of the general condition that led up to the outbreak. . . .

Four weeks spent in studying the situation in Chicago, immediately following the outbreaks, seem to show at least eight general causes for the riots, and the same conditions, to a greater or lesser degree, can be found in almost every large city with an appreciable Negro population. These causes, taken after a careful study in order of their prominence, are

1. Race Prejudice
2. Economic Competition
3. Political Corruption and Exploitation of Negro Voters
4. Police Inefficiency
5. Newspaper Lies about Negro Crime
6. Unpunished Crimes against Negroes
7. Housing

8. Reaction of Whites and Negroes from War

Some of these can be grouped under the same headings, but due to the prominence of each they are listed as separate causes.

Prior to 1915, Chicago had been famous for its remarkably fair attitude toward colored citizens. Since that time, when the migratory movement from the South assumed large proportions, the situation has grown steadily more and more tense. This was due in part to the introduction of many Negroes who were unfamiliar with city ways and could not, naturally, adapt themselves immediately to their new environment. . . . But equally important, though seldom considered, is the fact that many Southern whites have also come into the North, many of them to Chicago, drawn by the same economic advantages that attracted the colored workmen. . . . These have spread the virus of race hatred and evidence of it can be seen in Chicago on every hand. This same cause underlies each of the other seven causes.

With regard to economic competition, the age-long dispute between capital and labor enters. Large numbers of Negroes were brought from the South by the packers and there is little doubt that this was done in part so that the Negro might be used as a club over the head of the unions. . . . On the other hand, the Negro workman is not at all sure as to the sincerity of the unions themselves. . . . The Negro is between "the devil and the deep blue sea." He feels that if he goes into the unions, he will lose the friendship of the employers. He knows that if he does not, he is going to be met with the bitter antagonism of the unions. . . .

There is probably no city in America with more of political trickery, chicanery and exploitation than Chicago. Against the united and bitter opposition of every major daily newspaper in Chicago, William Hale Thompson was elected again as mayor, due, as was claimed, to the Negro and German vote. While it is not possible to state that the anti-Thompson element deliberately brought on the riots, yet it is safe to say that they were not adverse to its coming. . . .

The fourth contributing cause was the woeful inefficiency and criminal negligence of the police authorities of Chicago, both prior to and during the riots. . . .

During the riots the conduct of the police force as a whole was open to criticism. State's attorney Hoyne openly charged the police with arresting colored rioters and with an unwillingness to arrest white rioters. Those who were arrested were at once released. In one case a colored man who was fair enough to appear to be white was arrested for carrying concealed weapons, together with five white men and a number of colored men. All were taken to a police station; the light colored man and the five whites being put into one cell and the other colored men in another. In a few minutes the light colored man and the five whites were released and their ammunition given back to them with the remark, "You'll probably need this before the night is over."

Fifth on the list is the effect of newspaper publicity concerning Negro crime. With the exception of the *Daily News*, all of the papers of Chicago have played up in prominent style with glaring, prejudice-breeding headlines every crime or suspected crime committed by Negroes. Headlines such as NEGRO BRUTALLY MURDERS PROMINENT CITIZEN, NEGRO ROBS HOUSE and the like have appeared with alarming frequency and the news articles beneath such headlines have been of the same sort. During the rioting such headlines as NEGRO BANDITS TERRORIZE TOWN, RIOT- ERS BURN 100 HOMES—NEGROES SUSPECTED OF HAVING PLOT- TED BLAZE appeared. As can easily be seen such newspaper accounts did not tend to lessen the bitterness of feeling between the conflicting groups. . . .

For a long period prior to the riots, organized gangs of white hoodlums had been perpetrating crimes against Negroes for which no arrests had been made. These gangs in many instances masqueraded under the name of "Ath- letic and Social Clubs" and later direct connection was shown between them and incendiary fires started during the riots. Colored men, women, and chil- dren had been beaten in the parks, most of them in Jackson and Lincoln Parks. In one case a young colored girl was beaten and thrown into a lagoon. In other cases Negroes were beaten so severely that they had to be taken to hospitals. All of these cases have caused many colored people to wonder if they could expect any protection whatever from the authorities. . . .

Much has been written and said concerning the housing situation in Chi- cago and its effect on the racial situation. The problem is a simple one. Since 1915 the colored population of Chicago has more than doubled. . . . Most of them lived in the area bounded by the railroad on the west, 30th Street on the north, 40th Street on the south and Ellis Avenue on the east. Already overcrowded, this so-called "Black Belt" could not possibly hold the doubled colored population. . . . [A] hysterical group of persons formed "Property Owners Associations" for the purpose of trying to keep intact white neighborhoods. . . .

In a number of cases during the period from January 1918, to August, 1919, there were bombings of colored homes and houses occupied by Negroes outside of the "Black Belt." During this period no less than twenty bombings took place, yet only two persons have been arrested and neither of the two has been convicted, both cases being continued.

Finally the new spirit aroused in Negroes by their war experiences enters into the problem. From Local Board No. 4, embracing the neighborhood in the vicinity of State and 35th Streets, containing over 30,000 inhabitants of which fully ninety percent are colored, over 9,000 men registered and 1,850 went to camp. These men, with their new outlook on life, injected the same spirit of independence into their companions, a thing that is true of many other sections of America. One of the greatest surprises to many of those who came down to "clean out the niggers" is that the same "niggers" fought back. Colored men saw their own kind being killed, heard of many more and believed that their lives and liberty were at stake. In such a spirit most of the fighting was done.

f. Handwritten letter from S. H. Tarbet, Topeka, Kansas, to *The Crisis*, July 4, 1920

Now please do not use names of those who give out this. I have promised as much.

Arkansas mob Trouble and the truth of the affair. 12 men waiting for death while 80 to 90 are being held in Prison. By false accuasion by white men who done the killing.

The following is the substance of a letter wrote to a friend here in Topeka. From seas of the Trouble I think same should be investigated parties furnishing Information do not want their names mentioned so please do not use their names nor the names of one that furnished information. S. H. Tarbet 201 Jackson st. write me on this as I want to know how you feel about putting Bro White on this Case if he is not to well known there. I think all papers in union aught to have these facts.

A white man known to the Colored People on the Ration Plantation as Dug. Has a Colored woman for a mistress he tells his mistress one Blackwell owner of a big Plantation. D. Campbell Johnie Campbell. Clawrence Campbell Bosses on Ratio Plantation J. J. Petro Agent on Ratio plantation one Countress owner of store at same place Ratio one Stevenson that work around Hotel. one Sanders Book Keeper at Ratio Plantation store and man by name Willard who runs store at Elane along with 25 or 30 more white men went to Church at Hoop Spur. Shot in Church. all Colored people run. While they were there on scene up drove an automobile Colored driver. they though them Colored men returning to Church. so they blazed away wounding the Colored man who Jumped out of machine and run. Killed Agent and other man and wounded Deputy Sheriff of Course you may all ready have this information but do not use Hills or His mothers name. This was written Robt Hill now on bond to appear for trial before Judge Pollock in October. By his (Hills) mother says the mistress of this white man known as Dug. told her or that is the Sorce. Dougs mistress this come from. I think the Govinar. Atty general Arbuckle. and the rest of the officials of Arkansas and the Nation should know these facts. and turn those men out and bring guilty parties to trial. I should Say Justice but I am reminded there is no Justice in Phylips County Arkansas Investigate and do not print my name

Tarbet

g. "Negro Intruder Lynched," *Vicksburg Herald* (Mississippi), May 15, 1919

Lloyd Clay, 24-year-old negro laborer, was roasted to death here shortly after 8:00 o'clock last night. He had been charged with entering the bedroom of Miss Lulu Belle Bishop, aged 19, and attempting to violate her.

At an early hour yesterday, Clay forced his way through a screened window and entered Miss Bishop's bedroom. The young lady shrieked for help and fought him. Her father, Charles Bishop, attempted to go to her assistance, but could not break the door, which had been locked from within. The negro became alarmed and escaped through a window.

Charles Gantt's bloodhounds were brought from Crystal Springs. The hounds made two runs. On the first, they lost the scent. On the second they ran within ten feet of Clay who was standing at the A&V Railroad Station, as though waiting for the train to Jackson. They bayed at him and he was taken to jail. The young lady was taken to the jail to identify him, but she was not certain as to his identity.

A mob of between 800 and 1,000 men and women soon descended on the Jail. Using rails for battering rams, they snatched the prisoner from the sheriff.

The negro was taken to the corner of Clay and Farmer Streets, covered with oil, set aflame and hoisted to an elm tree. As the flaming body was pulled aloft, a fusillade of shots was fired into the negro's frame. A stray bullet struck Charles Lancaster back of the left ear, fracturing his skull. He is in the Vicksburg sanitarium in serious condition. A collection is being taken up for Lancaster's family.

h. "Negro Was Lynched to Save White Woman's Secret Lover," *New York Age*, June 14, 1919

JACKSON, Miss., June 3—A reader of THE AGE residing here has just completed an investigation of the recent lynching of a colored man by the name of Clay, at Vicksburg, and as often is the case, an innocent Negro met death at the hands of white men.

Anent the Vicksburg outrage the writer says: "I have been told by responsible colored men that it is generally accepted now that the party who went into the young white woman's room was a white man with whom she had been on intimate terms. The white man had visited the girl and was heard leaving the house when a member of the family called out and wanted to know who was up in the room. Then she screamed.

"The white man had employed a colored chauffeur to bring him to Jackson, the same chauffeur who had taken the couple for midnight drives on other occasions, and who had driven them earlier on the night of the outrage. The white man got away.

"The police went to the chauffeur's house upon his return to Vicksburg from Jackson and arrested him along with two other colored men, and they were taken to Jackson for 'safe-keeping.' When the chauffeur told all he knew in connection with the case the authorities turned all three loose and ordered them to leave the country.

"The girl failed completely to identify her assailant, and stated positively that Clay was not the man. Her father likewise pleaded with the mob not to lynch Clay, saying he wanted no innocent man killed and that if he found the right party he would need no mob to handle the case for him. But the bloodthirsty violators of the law wanted to murder somebody and put Clay to death."

Chapter 2: Migrants North

The most important demographic change in the United States during the years 1880 to 1924 was a westward movement of European immigrants into American cities, and a movement of settlers onto the Great Plains. African Americans participated in this worldwide migration by leaving the rural South for Northern, and some Southern, cities. Just as America offered freedom, land, and opportunity to immigrants from abroad, so did the North beckon to rural Southern black people, especially after World War I and 1920s legislation cut off European immigration.

The Bureau of the Census chronicled the African American migration in a comprehensive 845-page report published in 1935. The report describes every aspect of black life, including statistics on demography, education, families, economics, health, and other matters. This section of documents (a–f) shows some of those reports. A careful look at the numbers suggests how much had changed and how much remained the same in different parts of the country. For example, Table 10 (document d) shows the rapid growth of black communities in the North. However, documents b and c show that the majority of black people still lived in Georgia, Mississippi, Alabama, and other Southern states.

Social statistics are always open to different interpretations. For example, the report on school attendance (document e) shows that in 1930 16.3 percent of Negroes were illiterate, but only 2.7 percent of whites were illiterate. Yet, in 1920, fully 22.9 percent of African Americans could not read. The interpretation of these statistics depends in part on the reader's outlook. Do the figures suggest mostly oppression, progress, or a mix of both to you?

The chart on occupations (document f) shows some important contrasts between the North and the South. The most important is the percentage of African Americans engaged in industry. Twice as many black people, by percentage, are engaged in industry in the North.

Two articles form the Memphis newspapers (documents g and h) show one reason that many African Americans left the South. Contrast what these articles in the white press say to what you have read in the text.

Sources

Charles E. Hall, *Negroes in the United States 1920–1932: Report of the U.S. Census.* New York: Arno Press and the *New York Times* (reprint), 1969.

"Lowry Enroute to Lynching," *Memphis News-Scimitar,* January 26, 1921.

"Lowry Roasted by Inches before Wife and Children," *Memphis Press,* January 27, 1921.

a. From U.S. Census Special Report, 1935

Table I, 1 (excerpt)
Negro, White, and Other Population of the United States, with
Decennial Increase: 1790 to 1930

Census Year	All classes	Negro Number	(Percent)	White	Other
1930	122,775,046	11,891,143	(9.7)	108,864,207	2,019,696
1920	105,710,620	10,463,131	(9.9)	94,120,374	1,127,115
1910	91,972,266	9,827,763	(10.7)	81,364,447	78,056
1900	75,994,575	8,833,994	(11.6)	66,809,196	351,385
1890	62,947,714	7,488,676	(11.9)	55,101,258	357,780
1880	50,155,783	6,580,793	(13.1)	43,402,970	172,020
1870	38,558,371	4,880,009	(12.7)	33,589,377	88,985
1860	31,443,321	4,441,830	(14.1)	26,922,537	78,954

b. From U.S. Census Special Report, 1935

Table I, 5
Rank of States in Negro, White, and Total Population, 1930

State	Negro Pop.	Rank of State in		
		Negro Pop.	White Pop.	Total Pop.
Georgia	1,071,125	1	19	14
Mississippi	1,009,718	2	31	23
Alabama	944,834	3	22	15
North Carolina	918,647	4	16	12
Texas	854,964	5	7	5
South Carolina	793,681	6	33	26
Louisiana	776,325	7	29	22
Virginia	650,165	8	21	20
Arkansas	478,463	9	26	25
Tennessee	477,646	10	17	16
Florida	431,829	11	30	31
Pennsylvania	431,257	12	2	2
New York	412,814	13	1	1
Illinois	326,672	14	3	3
Ohio	309,364	15	4	4
Maryland	276,379	16	27	28
Kentucky	226,040	17	15	17
Missouri	223,840	18	10	10
New Jersey	208,828	19	9	9
Oklahoma	172,193	20	18	21

c. MAP OF CENSUS FIGURES

d. From U.S. Census Special Report, 1935

Table 10, Urbanization
Cities Having a Negro Population of Ten Thousand or More in 1935, with Comparative Figures for 1920 and Percentage Increase in Black Population

City	1920	1930	Difference Number	Difference Percent	Percent of Total 1920	Percent of Total 1930
New York	152,467	327,706	175,239	115	2.7	4.7
Chicago	109,458	233,903	124,445	114	4.1	6.9
Philadelphia	134,220	219,599	85,370	64	7.4	11.3
Baltimore	108,322	142,106	33,784	31	14.8	17.7
Washington	109,966	132,068	94,446	20	25.1	27.1
New Orleans	100,930	129,632	89,262	28	26.1	28.3
Detroit	40,838	120,066	79,228	194	4.1	7.7
Birmingham	70,230	99,077	28,847	41	39.3	38.2
Memphis	61,181	96,550	35,369	17	37.7	38.1
St. Louis	69,854	93,580	23,726	34	9	11.4
Atlanta	62,796	90,075	27,279	43	31.3	38.3
Cleveland	34,451	71,899	37,448	109	4.3	8
Houston	33,960	63,337	29,377	87	24.6	21.7
Pittsburgh	37,725	54,983	17,258	47	6.4	8.2
Richmond	54,041	52,988	− 1,053	− 2	31.5	29
Jacksonville	41,520	48,196	6,676	16	45.3	37.2
Cincinnati	30,079	47,818	17,739	59	7.5	10.6
Louisville	40,087	47,354	7,267	18	17.1	15.4
Indianapolis	34,678	43,967	9,289	27	11	12.1
Norfolk	43,392	43,942	550	1	37.5	33.9

e. From U.S. Census Special Report, 1935

Illiteracy, Over 10 Years Old

	Total Number	Number Illiterate	Percent
1930			
All Classes	98,723,047	4,283,753	4.3
Negro	9,292,556	1,513,892	16.3
White	87,980,667	2,407,218	2.7

1920

All Classes	82,739,315	4,931,905	6.0
Negro	8,053,225	1,842,161	22.9
White	74,359,749	3,006,312	4.0

f. From U.S. Census Special Report, 1953

Occupations, 1930
Number (in Thousands) and Percentage Distribution of Workers, Ten Years Old and Over, and Percent Total of All Workers

Occupation	Total		Negro		Native White		% of Total	
	Number	(%)	Number	(%)	Number	(%)	Negro	Native White
Agriculture	10,472	(22)	1,988	(36)	7,519	(21)	19	72
Forestry	250	(0.5)	31	(0.6)	167	(0.5)	13	67
Mining	984	(2)	75	(1)	658	(2)	8	67
Manufacturing	14,110	(29)	1,025	(19)	9,664	(28)	7	69
Transportation	3,843	(8)	398	(7)	2,876	(8)	10	75
Trade	6,081	(12)	183	(3)	4,835	(14)	3	80
Public service	856	(2)	50	(1)	679	(2)	6	80
Professionals	3,254	(7)	136	(2.5)	2,775	(8)	4	85
Domestics	4,952	(10)	1,576	(29)	2,328	(7)	32	47
Clerical	4,025	(8)	41	(0.7)	3,672	(10)	1	91

g. "Lowry Enroute to Lynching," *Memphis News-Scimitar*, January 26, 1921

MILLINGTON, Tenn., Jan. 26—A party of seven in two automobiles, with Henry Lowry, negro murderer, stopped here at 12:30 o'clock this after-noon. The party is en route from Sardis, Miss., where they took the prisoner from officers, to Wilson, Ark., where Lowry is said to have murdered two members of the Craig family and where the party intends to lynch him.

The party stopped at Fowler's restaurant for lunch. The negro was taken into the restaurant and kept under observation while the party ate.

The negro said nothing, but showed the intense strain he was under. He realized he was on his way to death. A number of Millington citizens were attracted to the restaurant and conversed with him while the white men ate.

Nothing has occurred to mar the serenity of the party's journey. The party ate leisurely and after finishing went to F. A. Harrold's store, where a quantity of rope was purchased.

h. "Lowry Roasted by Inches before Wife and Children," *Memphis Press*, January 27, 1921

NODENA, Ark., Jan. 27—"Cap, I want to be buried at Magnolia, Miss." These were the last words spoken by Henry Lowry, negro murderer, who was burned at the stake last night, three-quarters of a mile east of here.

More than 500 persons stood by and looked on while the negro was slowly burned to a crisp. A few women were scattered among the crowd of Arkansas planters who directed the gruesome work of avenging the deaths of O. T. Craig and his daughter, Mrs. C. O. Williamson. Among those in the crowd were Lowry's tearful wife and children.

The setting was a natural amphitheater between two bluffs, with the Mississippi River on one side and a huge lake, created by backwater, on the other. The negro was chained to a log. Members of the mob placed a small pile of dry leaves around his feet. Gasoline was then poured onto the leaves, and the carrying out of the death sentence was under way.

Inch by inch the negro was fairly cooked to death. Lowry retained consciousness for forty minutes. Not once did he whimper or beg for mercy.

As flesh began to drop away from his legs and they were reduced to bones, once or twice he attempted to pick up hot coals and swallow them in order to hasten death. Each time the coals were kicked from his grasp by members of the mob.

As the flames reached his abdomen, two men closed in on him and began to question him. The slayer answered their questions freely and the general impression was that he was telling the truth when he admitted his guilt in killing the man on whose farm he was a tenant and his daughter.

A big six-footer put the questions to the condemned man, while another wrote the answers down in a note book. It resembled a courtroom scene, with prosecuting attorney and court reporter. Other members of the mob crowded around, but not once did they attempt to interrogate the negro, leaving this to the pair who appeared to have been assigned this duty.

Words fail to describe the sufferings of the negro. Yet only once did he cry out. This was shortly before he lost consciousness as flames began to lick at his chest and face. He cried out some appeal to one of the many negro lodges of which he was a member.

Then gasoline was poured over his head and it was only a few minutes until he had been reduced to ashes.

After Lowry had been reduced to a charred mass, members of the mob headed in the direction of Osceola. It was whispered that they were planning to raid the jails at Marion and Blytheville in order to secure possession of five more negroes, in order to raise the total number lynched to an even half dozen.

The mob, after riding back and forth across the country for several hours, finally began to disperse and go home. It was evident that the leaders were practically exhausted from their long trip with Lowry.

Chapter 3: Changing Institutions in Changing Times

Segregation forced African Americans to develop their own separate institutions. In religion, business, labor, women's rights, education, social services, and other areas, African Americans organized a nation within a nation. Some enterprises were national in scope and existed in hundreds of communities, while others were unique to a locality. Taken together, they made "African America" a separate place.

Religious and social institutions made a place feel like home for new migrants and old settlers. There is no mistaking the sense of "arrival" conveyed by the magnificent new quarters of the Abyssinian Baptist Church in Harlem (document a). Similarly, the festivities at the Alpha Phi Alpha Fraternity convention show pride in the achievements of Paul Laurence Dunbar (document b). The advertisements for schools and colleges (document c) are typical of those found in the African American press of the 1920s.

New businesses were another source of pride. A selection of advertisements from *The Crisis* magazine (documents d–f) gives a sense of what goods and services black people produced in the 1920s. The National Benefit Life Insurance Company provided black people with a necessary service while at the same time becoming a source of pride. Some ads, like that for Black Swan Records, proudly announce the race of the singers, while Madame C. J. Walker's products on this list might be used by anyone.

However, the necessity for separate social organizations linked to wider struggles had to provoke a certain sense of anger, as well as pride, among 1920s African Americans. Some organizations black people formed of necessity. Black workers might have belonged to integrated trade unions, but white workers would not have them. In fact, as "Midnight Terrorists," shows, white workers forced black men into low-skill jobs, sometimes killing those who stood up for their rights (document g). In "The New Pullman Porter," A. Philip Randolph argues that the porters would no longer meekly accept whatever the Pullman Company offered them (document h). The new union ultimately won a contract and became a leading instrument of civil rights struggle in the 1930s.

Just as white workers kept black men out of their organizations, so did white women. An unsigned article from *The Crisis* on the International Council of Women reveals the segregationist views of white Southern women toward African American women (document i). Jessie Fauset's report on the National Association of Colored Women shows how it spoke up for women in general and participated in the movement for racial justice (document j). John Hope stresses the gains in interracial understanding made by the colored YMCA (document k). Yet, the very fact that whites insisted upon racially separate organizations showed how segregated America was in the 1920s.

Sources

"Abyssinian Church of New York" (September 1923), "Fraternity and Sorority News" (March 1924), "International Council of Women" (December 1920), "The 13th Biennial of the NACW" (October 1922), and "The Colored Y.M.C.A." (November 1925) first appeared in *The Crisis*. The author wishes to thank the Crisis Publishing Company, the publisher of the magazine of the NAACP, for the use of these articles.

"The New Pullman Porter," *Messenger*, April 1926.

"Midnight Terrorists Lynch Negro Brakeman on the Y&MV," *Memphis Times-Scimitar*, March 18, 1921.

a. "The Abyssinian Church of New York," *The Crisis*, September 1923

One of the greatest signs of progress among colored Americans has been their realization that the church should be the center not only of religious but also of social and community activities. The new buildings of the Abyssinian Baptist Church in New York have been constructed with this idea in mind.

Abyssinian Church was organized 115 years ago and is the third oldest Baptist Church in America. Its first edifice was on Worth Street in New York, a far cry from its present location in Harlem. Fifteen ministers have presided over it and it boasts a long line of progressive leaders and faithful communicants. To-day its membership is nearly 4,000.

While it is true that this organization has always been outstanding among Negro Churches, it began to gain new prominence about fifteen years ago when the Reverend A. Clayton Powell came from New Haven, Connecticut to assume its pastorate. This pastor, a graduate of Virginia Union University and of Yale Divinity School has always had a great interest in social problems and he has known how to introduce a larger vision of social service into the administration of his church. The new Abyssinian Church and Community House are the outgrowth of this vision.

The buildings are situated on 138th Street with a frontage of 150 feet. They are among the most modern and valuable church holdings in America. Their total cost amounts to $325,000. It is significant of the increasing prosperity among colored people to learn that $265,000 of this amount was raised and paid before the church was dedicated.

b. "Fraternity and Sorority News," *The Crisis*, March 1924

The 16th Annual Convention of the Alpha Phi Alpha Fraternity was held at the seat of Kappa Chapter, Columbus, Ohio, from December 27th to the 31st. The convention headquarters was the large and newly constructed Y. M. C. A. on Spring Street. The citizens of Columbus as well as the members of Kappa Chapter worked unceasingly to attend to the needs and comfort of the large number of delegates and visiting brothers present.

Founded at Cornell University in 1907, this organization has now 51 undergraduate and graduate chapters and a total membership of about 3,000. Its chapters extend from Harvard in the East to the University of California and as far south as Atlanta University at Atlanta, Georgia. Among the fraternity members are some of the race leaders along educational and scientific lines.

Many social functions were given by the citizens and clubs of Columbus during the meeting of the Fraternity. The fact that the annual convention of the Delta Sigma Theta Sorority was held in Columbus at the same time added materially to the social life of the two meetings.

The chief social event was the annual "Formal" of the Fraternity held in the gymnasium of the Ohio State University on Friday evening, December 28th. The large gymnasium was handsomely decorated with orange and black, the colors of the fraternity, intermingled with the banners of the different colleges represented. About two hundred couples were present and danced until 2 A.M. to the strains from a palm-screened orchestra placed in the center of the gymnasium.

The most outstanding event of the convention was the pilgrimage on Sunday, December 30, to Dayton, Ohio, to the home of Paul Laurence Dunbar, under the direction of Theta Lambda chapter of Dayton. Two special cars conveyed the delegates and their friends to Dayton. There they were met by autos and taken to the home of Dunbar where appropriate exercises were held. The principal speech here was by Raymond C. Cannon of Minneapolis, general Vice-President of the Middle West.

From the house the delegates were driven to the grave of Dunbar where they held an impressive ceremony under the direction of the general President of the Fraternity, S. S. Booker, of Baltimore, Maryland. After the exercises at the grave the delegates and their friends were driven to Memorial Hall where a dinner was tendered by Theta Lambda Chapter assisted by the citizens of Dayton. About five hundred attended. During the dinner musical selections were rendered by the Harry T. Burleigh Glee-Club of Dayton, by Mrs. Handy of Columbus and Miss Helen of Cincinnati. Selections from Dunbar were rendered during the several exercises by Miss Edna Browne of Dayton.

c. Crisis Educational Institution Ads

d. through f. *Crisis* Ads

g. "Midnight Terrorists Lynch Negro Brakeman on the Y&MV," *Memphis Times-Scimitar*, March 18, 1921

LAKE CORMORANT, Miss., Mar. 17—A series of warnings by masked white men to negro brakemen of the Yazoo and Mississippi Valley Railroad to quit their jobs was culminated by the lynching here last night of Howard Hurd, of Memphis. Hurd mysteriously disappeared from the freight train he was working when it was halted at Clayton, Miss., for a hot box. He was found riddled with bullets 500 yards north of the Lake Cormorant station at 5 o'clock this morning. The following note was found in his overalls:

"Take this as a warning to all nigger railroad men."

Hurd had been employed by the Yazoo and Mississippi for several years. For the past five weeks negro brakemen have been terrorized by gangs of white men who stop Y&MV trains between Memphis and Clarksdale, Miss., and molest them. Several negro trainmen have been severely beaten. . . .

The method of the midnight terrorists, it is said, is to ride freight trains out of Memphis, or to board them at points south of here. When the trains reach points where they want to take the negro brakemen off, the angle cock is opened, throwing on the air brakes the entire length of the train. The masked men seem to know the location of the negro brakemen, and take them quickly, and without commotion.

They are said never to be seen by the white members of the crews who will have nothing to say about the mysterious occurrences. . . .

Several negro railroad men are expected to leave the road, due to the murder of Hurd.

h. "The New Pullman Porter," by A. Philip Randolph, *Messenger*, April 1926

A new Pullman porter is born. He breathes a new spirit. He has caught a new vision. His creed is independence without insolence; courtesy without fawning; service without servility. His slogan is: "Opportunity not alms." For a fair day's work, he demands a fair day's wage. He reasons that if it is just and fair and advantageous for the Pullman Company to organize in order to sell service to the traveling public, that it is also just and fair and advantageous for the porters to organize in order to sell their service to the Pullman Company; that if it is to the best interests of the Pullman Conductors to form an organization of, by and for themselves, it is to the best interests of the Pullman porters to form an organization of, by and for themselves. He has learnt from experience that the Company Union sugar-coated the Employee Representation Plan cannot and will not serve his interests any more than it can or will serve the interests of the Pullman conductors, the engineers, switchmen, firemen, train conductors or trainmen. He has common sense enough to sense the fact that the Plan is the darling creature of the Company, hatched and nourished for the benefit of the Company, not the porter; that he can no more get justice at its hands than could a rat get justice before a jury of cats. His doctrine is that the best kind of help is self-help expressed through organized action.

The new Pullman porter is a rebel against all that the "Uncle Tom" idea suggests. The former possesses the psychology of let well enough alone. The latter that of progressive improvement. The former relies upon charity and pity; the latter upon his intelligence, initiative and thrift. The old time porter is afflicted with an inferiority complex; the new porter logically takes the position that a man's worth in society is not the result of race, color, creed or nationality; but that a man's worth is based upon the quality of his service to society.

The old time porter assumed that a clownal grin or a "buck and wing" was a necessary part of the service in order to extract a dime tip from an amused and oft-times a disgusted passenger; whereas, the new porter believes that intelligence and dignity and industry are the chief factors in service of quality and value. As a service agent, the new porter seeks to anticipate the desires of his passengers with a view to making their travel ideal. He realizes that his service is a representative form of salesmanship for the Company to the public, and for himself to the Company and the public. His work is not alone regulated by the mechanical requirements of the service, but out of his rich and full experience, he is ever formulating new and higher forms of service. Many constructive and practical ideas lie in the heads of porters who are reluctant to reveal them because they feel that they neither get the proper appreciation or reward from the Company for them. A just wage stimulates the employees to give their best to their employer; it develops a larger interest in the job and a joy in performing a high type of workmanship.

The new porter is not amenable to the old slave-driving methods, his best service is secured through an appeal to his intelligence. Just as he demands fairer treatment than the old time porter, for the same reason, he gives a higher type of service. Just as he rejects charity and pity on the grounds that he is a man, and doesn't need such, so he refuses to make excuses, but performs his duties in accordance with the requirements of efficient service.

His object is not only to get more wages, better hours of work and improved working conditions, but to do his bit in order to raise and progressively improve the standard of Pullman service. The new Pullman porter takes the position that his ability to render the Company increased productive efficiency can only result from his increased physical, moral and mental efficiency, which rest directly upon a higher standard of living, which in turn, can only be secured by a higher, regular income. His insistence upon a regular, living wage is based upon the fact that not only is the tipping system morally unjustifiable, but because tips fluctuate violently in amounts, from month to month, and a porter is for ever uncertain as to how to regulate his household affairs, since he cannot definitely plan on how much money he can spend above his meager wage of $67.50 a month, on his wife's clothing, furniture for his home, or his children's education. No other group of workers are required to work under such distracting uncertainty. Of course, the reason is that they are organized.

The new Pullman porter believes in organization and is wont to convince the Company and the traveling public that the Brotherhood will be a distinct asset to the Pullman industry in the practical and efficient handling of service and personel problems. He is cognizant of the fact that the security and well-fare of the porters are bound up with the steady, continued and sustained progress of the Pullman industry. He is confident that his experience in the service equips, adapts and furnishes him with a peculiar and unique type of training and knowledge which no other employee possesses, and, therefore, renders him highly capable of giving constructive cooperation to the Company which will reflect itself in better service, and, hence better business.

The new porter is not a Communist, but a simple trade unionist, seeking only to become a better and a more useful citizen by securing a higher standard of living and preserving his manhood.

i. "The International Council of Women," *The Crisis*, December 1920

The International Council of Women meets every five years. This year it met in Christiania, Norway, and for the first time had an accredited Negro delegate, Mrs. Mary B. Talbert of Buffalo, N. Y., and her alternate, Dr. Mary F. Waring of Chicago. The race has been represented unofficially twice before—by Miss Hallie Q. Brown who addressed the London meeting in 1899 and by Mrs. Mary Church Terrell who spoke at the Berlin meeting in 1904.

The delegates, including Mrs. Talbert and her daughter and Dr. Waring, traveled in a party via Italy, Switzerland, France, Belgium, Denmark, Norway and Scotland. There were five southern-born white women in the party: Mrs. Alexander Watkins of Minter City, Miss.; Mrs. James Riley of Charlotte, N. C., former vice-president of the General Federation of Women's Clubs; Mrs. O. J. Chandler of Harrodsburg, Ky.; Mrs. Heisey of Great Falls, Mont.; and Mrs. Marsh of Wyoming. These women together with Mrs. Howard Gould during the whole 78 days of the journey made the life of the colored delegates as uncomfortable as possible. Mrs. Gould began the campaign on shipboard by repeating in a loud voice various tales of the systematic importation of southern colored women into the North for voting purposes. Repeated efforts were made to segregate the colored women in Italy and Switzerland. At the American Y. W. C. A. in Paris, where the party arrived late in the morning after an all night ride, all the white delegates were welcomed and accommodated while the colored delegates were even refused breakfast. At Antwerp, Mrs. Riley went to the proprietor of the hotel and demanded segregation of the colored guests, which he refused. Mrs. Watkins left the party at Brussels to avoid further contact.

In Birmingham, England, at the Queen's Hotel, Mrs. Heisey and Mrs. Riley refused seats at the table where Mrs. Talbert and her daughter were sitting and left the dining-room. At Copenhagen, Denmark, they were entertained at the American Consul. Mrs. Gould, Mrs. Chandler and Mrs. Marsh, of Wyoming, refused to attend because the colored women were there.

At the meeting of the council the colored women received every courtesy from the foreign delegates and from the American officials, Mrs. Philip North Moore and Mrs. Joseph C. Merriman. During this time Mrs. Talbert published four articles on our race problem in two leading Christiania papers.

On the return there were several social functions of such importance that the Southerners were compelled to endure in silence the presence of the colored delegates. For instance, all the delegates were entertained by the King and Queen of Norway. All the Southerners were present. Lady Aberdeen, president of the Council, entertained the delegates and alternates at breakfast. Mrs. Riley was placed opposite Dr. Waring and did not leave the table. At Hadow House, Aberdeen, Scotland, on the way back, Lady Aberdeen entertained the whole American party. At her request Mrs. Talbert sat at her right and the representative of the Jewish women, Mrs. Nathan Harris, at her left. All the Southerners were present. Mrs. Riley sat at the right of Lord Aberdeen and Mrs. Merriman, conductor of the party, on the left. They were entertained at Edinburgh, Scotland, by the Common Council. All were present.

And so the eventful journey ended with the colored women quietly and with dignity standing at their guns and the southern white women furious at the "social equality!"

j. "The 13th Biennial of the N.A.C.W.," *The Crisis*, October 1922

My attendance on the thirteenth biennial session of the National Association of Colored Women left me tingling, one might almost say, bristling, with impressions. There were so many different angles from which to receive them. And as this was my first visit to such a convention and also my first trip south of Washington, I was peculiarly susceptible.

Picture a group of women with a nucleus of 466 delegates, constantly being enlarged by visitors and interested spectators and you have the first idea of the convention which met during the week of August 6, in Richmond, Va. There were literally all sorts of colored women there—black, white, brown, tall and short, portly and slender. Most of them registered a high average of intelligence and a striking knowledge of parliamentary law. Some represented the highest grade of mentality. All were alert, thoughtful and interested.

The president of the N. A. C. W. is Miss Hallie Q. Brown, of Wilberforce, Ohio. In a comprehensive opening address she laid special stress on the relation of the N. A. C. W. to woman suffrage. "This organization," she declared, "should be the school-mistress to teach proper use of the ballot; to teach us to study situations and conditions that we may vote wisely for our best interests; and that those who have the ballot may help those denied this right; to this end we have organized everywhere civic clubs to combat indifference, ignorance, and exploitation of the Negro woman's vote."

The evening sessions were thrown open to the public at large, and several remarkable and enlightening addresses were delivered. But the real work of the association was done in the days which were filled with business. The constitution was completely revised and an election of officers held. . . .

Of course all this was purely routine business. The purpose of the organization showed itself in the activities of the departmental workers of the N. A. C. W. who by demonstration, discussion, lectures, and delivery of papers presented their special interests to the audience. Many of these departmental leaders had secured the services of men and women who had made a special study of some peculiar activity and who were able therefore to speak with authority. . . .

The departments whose work was presented were those of needlework, fine arts, forestry, social science, associated charities, juvenile court, eugenics, home economics, literature, lynching, defense, health and hygiene, neighborhood union, colored business women, industry, scholarship, peace and foreign relations, moral standards and citizenship.

At evening meetings Mr. James Weldon Johnson and Mr. Walter P. White, of the N. A. A. C. P., spoke with precision and passion on the anti-lynching bill; Mr. N. D. Brascher, editor of the Associated Negro Press, discussed "The Press and Publicity for Club Workers"; Mrs. Margaret Peak Hill, of Baltimore, spoke of the work of the W. C. T. U. against the evils of tobacco and liquor; Mrs. F. R. Givens of Louisville, Ky., Mrs. Casely Hayford of Sierra

Leone, and Miss Jessie Fauset, spoke on Africa. The latter interpreted the meaning of the Pan-African Congress; Mrs. Givens recounted the experiences gained recently on her six months' tour of West Africa; and Mrs. Hayford in native costume gave her hearers information at first hand about the needs of African women. The audience responded to her with a generous gift of $154 for the school which she plans to start on her return to Africa in October.

The political note was again sounded at the final evening meeting by Mrs. Dodson of Iowa, who represented the National Woman's Republican League, and by Mrs. Isabella Kendig-Gill, of the National Woman's Party, who stressed the economic, property and parental rights of women. . . .

The National Association of Colored Women has its hand in all possible activities concerning colored people, from the welfare of the smallest dark orphan in Texas to the fate of the Anti-Lynching Bill in the Senate. It is a great and far-reaching organization with immense possibilities.

k. "The Colored Y.M.C.A.," *The Crisis*, November 1925

In the City of Washington in the month of October was held the National Y. M. C. A. Conference on the Colored Work. Delegates from all parts of the United States attended. White and colored leaders in Y. M. C. A. work at home and in foreign countries were present. This was a deliberative assembly. The usual set speeches, in the main, gave place to an earnest inquiry into what the Colored Y. M. C. A. is, what is its present field, how is it functioning in this field, what new fields may it enter and how shall all this be accomplished. No meeting in the interest of Y. M. C. A. work among colored people has ever been approached with higher hopes, more serious purpose and greater sense of responsibility than this.

In such quiet and orderly manner has the Y. M. C. A. done its work among colored men that many may not realize its present proportions. But there are 140 Y. M. C. A. Associations in colored schools and colleges and 68 city, railroad, town and country centers. This work extends from New York to Los Angeles and is in many places in the South. Last year Y. M. C. A. dormitories supplied 446,000 lodgings, served 302,000 meals, had 81,500 men and boys attending Bible classes and 285,000 attending other religious meetings. There were 1578 young colored men and boys led to a Christian decision and church membership, while 1089 were led to enter Christian callings as a life work. There are 16 modern buildings, 14 of which are standard buildings, and the property in use for Y. M. C. A. work among colored men amounts to several million dollars. . . .

But this is not all that the colored Y. M. C. A. indicates. From the very first there has been an equality even where at times separation has existed; and considering some of the sad traditions and circumstances of interracial endeavor probably no organization stands out for greater fairness and affords a finer brotherhood than the Y. M. C. A. Perhaps the beginnings of a more modern interracial endeavor was inspired by Y. M. C. A leadership, and the improved understanding and enlarged sympathy existing today between white and colored students in the South is traceable directly to the planning of the Y. M. C. A.

Discrimination, injustice and a lack of much that makes other people prosperous have a tendency to draw the victim of these into himself, and much that Negroes do necessarily has to be a measure of self-relief. But the Y. M. C. A. makes the effort to open up to Negro youth the world as his field. It urges young Negroes to attend student volunteer meetings and many other gatherings where the world is spread out before the gaze of youth. In this way Max Yergan became the first Negro missionary to the Indian in Asia where he received a training that has made him the successful pioneer Y. M. C. A. missionary among the youth in Africa where he now lives and works; and many another youth is looking to Africa as a place to invest his life in the reclamation of the world through Jesus Christ.

The problem of Negro youth in the hours when he is not at work has not been adequately met and no organization in America is so well prepared to meet it as the colored Y. M. C. A. Boys' work men are needed in many centers and it may be that the colored Y. M. C. A. will have to carry on much more work where standard buildings are not to be obtained.

Africa makes an appeal so momentous that it appalls even while it inspires. The way must be opened by governments and churches for the American colored man to do his part in improving the lives and saving the souls of millions of Negroes.

Chapter 4: Civil Rights

Civil rights activists campaigned to end lynching, segregation, and disfranchisement during the 1920s. Each of these evils posed complicated strategic problems that provoked discussion. Activists also debated how to participate in politics, especially since the Ku Klux Klan had taken over some Northern Republican parties. The documents in this section, grouped by issue, suggest what civil rights activists did in the 1920s.

The first newspaper articles here report on one notoriously barbaric lynching of three innocent men at Kirvin, Texas (documents a-c). As the third story shows, white men committed the crime for which the victims were burnt alive. During the fight for the Dyer antilynching bill, the NAACP gave reports of the lynching to every member of Congress (document d). *The Crisis* sounds a hopeful note for the bill's prospects in the Senate, but Southern Democrats blocked it (document d).

Selected articles from *The Crisis* show how independent activists fought against different aspects of segregation. The Springfield, Ohio, case describes a divided black community that nonetheless prevented legalized segregation (document f). J. H. Roberts conducted a successful "freedom ride" in interstate travel in 1923 (document g). The most notorious segregation case of the day occurred after Dr. Ossian Sweet moved into a white Detroit neighborhood. Someone in his house killed a white man who attacked the building with a mob. James Weldon Johnson describes the tense courtroom atmosphere at the second trial, in which Clarence Darrow, the most famous lawyer of the time, defending Ossian's brother Henry Sweet (document h).

Violent whites did whatever they could to keep black voters away from the polls. An account in the *New Republic* describes Election Day 1920 in Jacksonville and Ocoee, Florida (document i). In Texas, the legislature permitted a "white only" Democratic primary. Dr. Lawrence A. Nixon challenged this law in court. Justice Oliver Wendell Holmes ruled in a Supreme Court case that the law violated the Constitution, but Texas lawmakers later rewrote the law (document j). The battle raged on until World War II, when the Supreme Court ended the practice for good.

During the 1920s, the Ku Klux Klan reemerged as a force in American politics. The article by "A Kluxer" in the *Messenger* was probably written by Phillip Schuyler, a master of satire (document k). W. E. B. DuBois wrote the stirring "Manifesto of the Second Pan-African Congress" in 1921 (document l). It calls for the equality of races and the beginning of self-government by the colonial peoples of Africa. In this sense, the document looks forward to the independence of African nations, which was mostly achieved in the decades following World War II.

Sources

"Despite Lynching, 5 More Are Seized for Same Crime," *New York Call*, May 29, 1922.

"Triple Lynching Follows Thrilling Tex. Man-Hunt," *Brooklyn Citizen*, May 6, 1922.

"Sheriff Holds 2 Whites in Crime That 3 Burned For," *New York Call*, May 7, 1922.

"The Dyer Bill" (September 1922), "Springfield, Ohio, Defeats Segregated School Move" and "Interstate Passenger Wins Suit against Railroad"

(May 1923), "Detroit" (July 1926), and "Lynching" (January 1927) first appeared in *The Crisis*. The author wishes to thank the Crisis Publishing Company, the publisher of the magazine of the NAACP, for the use of this work.

Walter F. White, "Election by Terror in Florida," *New Republic*, January 12, 1921.

Nixon v. Herndon, 273 U.S. 536 (1927).

"America's Greatest Institution: The Ku Klux Klan," *Messenger*, April 1926.

W. E. B. DuBois, "Manifesto of the Second Pan-African Congress," *The Crisis*, November 1921,

a. "Despite Lynching, 5 More Are Seized for Same Crime," *New York Call*, May 29, 1922

WACO, Tex., May 28—Jesse Thomas, Negro, who was burned at the stake by a mob here Friday, may not have been the man who murdered Harrel Belton and assaulted his girl companion, authorities feared yesterday, and five other Negroes will be held in jail until further investigation has been made.

Officers were trying to link the murder of Belton with two other unsolved crimes committed here recently.

b. "Triple Lynching Follows Thrilling Tex. Man-Hunt," *Brooklyn Citizen*, May 6, 1922

KIRVIN, Tex., May 6—Three colored men were burned here at dawn for the murder of Eula Ausley, pretty 17-year-old school girl, whose body was found near here yesterday with thirty stab wounds. The three men were tied, one after another, to the seat of a cultivator, driven into the center of the city square and burned before a mob of 500.

"Shap" Curry, 26, Mose Jones, 44, and John Cornish, 19, were the victims. All three worked on the huge ranch of John King, the girl's grandfather. Curry was burned first. There was some delay in starting inasmuch as the men maintained their innocence to the last. Third degree methods failed to bring confessions.

The men were not shot but their bodies were mutilated prior to burning. Ears, toes and fingers were snipped off. Eyes were gouged out, no organ of the negroes was allowed to remain protruding.

After this preliminary mob vengeance, preachers from the two churches which flank the square came forward and prayed for the salvation of the blacks' souls.

As Curry was saturated with oil and set aflame, he chanted over and over again, "O Lord, I'm acomin." As the flames mounted about his body, his chant rose higher and higher until he could be heard throughout the down-town part of town. Curry lost consciousness in ten minutes and died.

Jones was then roped and dragged over the hot coals and more wood was thrown on. In six minutes, he, too, was dead. Cornish received the same treatment. Still more fuel was added and the three bodies were roasted in a bonfire that was kept going for six hours.

The lynchings followed one of the most thrilling man hunts in the history of these parts. Farmers and business men of three counties joined together to comb every inch of the territory. Creek bottoms were beaten all day and acres of grassland were flattened. Finally the three men were captured and brought to Fairfield where a mob gathered and took them from the sheriff after storming the jail.

c. "Sheriff Holds 2 Whites in Crime That 3 Burned For," *New York Call*, May 7, 1922

FAIRFIELD, Tex., May 6—Cliff and Arnie Powell, two white men, were detained today for further questioning in connection with the murder of Eula Ausley, for which three negroes were burned at Kirvin this morning. Sheriff H. M. Mayo declared that tracks leading from the scene of the murder led to the home of the brothers.

"The shoes of the Powells fit the tracks," was the terse comment of the sheriff.

One of the brothers was arrested yesterday and the other surrendered after the mob had taken the Negroes from the jail here. Said the sheriff, "The King and Powell families had some kind of a fight some time ago, in which one of the Powells was badly cut. This is just another clue we are following up."

d. Report of the House Judiciary Committee on the anti-lynching bill, "The Dyer Bill," *The Crisis*, September 1922

The committee has devoted much time and earnest thought to the con-sideration of this bill and has reached the conclusion that as amended the bill is constitutional and should pass. That conclusion is reached by different processes of reasoning and by reliance on different provisions of the Consti-tution; but whatever process of reasoning is adopted or whatever provisions of the Constitution are relied on we hold that the proposed legislation is appropriate legislation to cure or prevent the evil of lynching wherever in the United States and subject to the jurisdiction thereof that evil exists or is committed.

White or black, all persons born or naturalized in the United States . . .
are citizens of the United States, and no state by affirmative legislative, judicial or executive action, or by failure, neglect, or refusal to act, may deprive
any person of life, liberty, or property without due process of law, or deny to
any person within its jurisdiction the equal protection of the laws. . . .

The proposed legislation is not, and should not be considered, in any
sense sectional. The evil it is designed to cure is not confined to any particular section or state. . . . This monstrous evil, which is a disgrace to the
Nation, we should strive to wipe out by a firm and just exercise of every legitimate power conferred upon and residing in the Federal Government. . . .

American citizenship is indeed a badge of honor; it should be and this bill
seeks to make it a shield of protection to every American citizen, man,
woman and child.

e. "Lynching" *The Crisis*, January 1927
The curve of lynching has gone up again. The figures are

1919: 83
1920: 65
1921: 64
1922: 61
1923: 28
1924: 16
1925: 18
1926: 31

In the years 1900–1919 the lowest number lynched in any one year was
forty-eight and the highest one hundred and eight. The crusade of the
N.A.A.C.P. started the awakening of the white South and brought the figures sharply down. In 1926 thirty-one have already been lynched as we go to
press.

f. "Springfield, Ohio, Defeats Segregated School Move," *The Crisis*, May
1923
AFTER a very lengthy and difficult fight, the colored citizens of Springfield, Ohio, have defeated an attempt to force segregated schools upon the
colored people of that city. The task was made more difficult because ministers of two of the largest churches of the city openly advocated the creation
of the separate school. The fight has extended over more than a year and was
conducted by the Springfield Branch of the N. A. A. C. P. and a General
Citizens Committee. Visits were made to Springfield by Field Secretaries
Hunton and Bagnall who aided in the laying of plans for the campaign

against this attempt. Meetings were held with the Board of Education when many petitions against the separate school were presented but with no success. Mass and committee meetings were held, parades were organized and the school was boycotted and picketed. Finally an injunction against the school was applied for, which was granted by the court, later being made permanent.

The citizens of Springfield are to be highly congratulated upon this determined fight to prevent encroaching attempts of segregation and discrimination which are being tried in numerous cities of the North and, particularly, in Ohio. It is hoped that the splendid example will have effect upon other cities where the colored citizens are not as awake to the danger as those in Springfield.

g. "Interstate Passenger Wins Suit against Railroad," *The Crisis*, May 1923.

AN important decision has just been rendered in a case affecting the right of a colored passenger in interstate traveling. Mr. J. H. Roberts, a colored man of St. Louis, purchased a ticket from St. Louis to McAlister, Oklahoma. He rode in a chair car as far as the Oklahoma state line when he was ordered to go forward to the Jim crow section of the train. Mr. Roberts refused to do so, citing the fact that he was an interstate passenger and therefore the separate coach law of Oklahoma did not apply to him. The Pullman porter who had ordered Mr. Roberts to move brought the conductor and the two of them forced Mr. Roberts to move.

Mr. Roberts returned to St. Louis and entered suit against the St. Louis, San Francisco Railway Company for $10,000. The case was tried before Judge Robert W. Hall of the Circuit Court sitting at St. Louis. The Railway Company in its defense relied upon the Oklahoma separate car law and upon the rules and regulations of the company. Messrs. Freeman L. Martin, George B. Jones and Frank S. Bledsoe, colored attorneys of St. Louis, contended on behalf of Mr. Roberts that he being an interstate passenger was not subjected to the Oklahoma Jim-crow law.

After hearing arguments and briefs on both sides, Judge Hall sustained a motion of the plaintiff and denied to the defense that the railway company had any right to force Mr. Roberts to ride in the Jim-crow car under the provisions of the Oklahoma Jim-crow law or the company's rules and regulations. Messrs. Martin, Jones and Bledsoe were aided in drawing their brief by Mr. James A. Cobb, Vice-dean of the Howard University Law School and attorney at Washington for the N. A. A. C. P. Judge Hall's decision is of great importance affecting as it does so fundamental a question.

h. "Detroit," *The Crisis*, July 1926, by James Weldon Johnson

For eight months the National Office has been steeped in the Sweet case. It has whipped up every energy and drawn upon every resource to carry the fight through to victory. All of us at the office realized the responsibility involved, and carried the whole matter on our hearts.

But when I entered the Recorder's Court of Detroit on Monday morning May 3, in the midst of the second trial, I felt myself thrust suddenly, as an individual, into an arena of vital conflict and personally engaged in the struggle. I was at once so gripped by the tense drama being enacted before my eyes that I became a part of the tragedy. And tragedy it was. The atmosphere was tragic. The serried rows of colored faces that packed the courtroom from the rail to the back wall, watching and waiting, were like so many tragic masks. The mild, soft-spoken boy being tried for murder in the first degree and, for the time, carrying the onus of the other ten defendants, and upon whose fate hung the right of the black man to defend himself in his home was an extremely tragic figure. The twelve white men sitting over against him, under oath to disregard prejudice and to render a true and just verdict between black and white in a land where race prejudice is far more vital than religion, also became tragic figures. The rugged face of Clarence Darrow, more haggard and lined by the anxious days, with the deep, brooding eyes, heightened the intense effect of the whole.

For a week I listened to testimony and the examination of witnesses. Each day the courtroom on the other side of the rail was packed as tightly as the space would permit. First, the witnesses for the prosecution, most of them members of the police force, evading the truth, distorting the truth, actually lying. And why? Because they were opposed to a Negro moving into a white neighborhood? Not primarily. The policemen who testified felt, even though a man's liberty was at stake, that they had to justify the course which the police had followed in the case. And so policeman after policeman, under oath, testified that, on the night of the shooting, the streets around the Sweet house were almost deserted. . . . And thus they showed themselves willing to swear away a man's liberty for life in order to save the face of the Police Department. . . .

The court reconvened. The judge ascended to the bench. . . . I sat next to Henry Sweet. I put my hand on his arm and said, "No matter what happens the National Association will stand by you to the end."

The jury was called in. They filed in solemnly and took their places facing the bench. The clerk asked, "Gentlemen, have you arrived at a verdict?" The answer was "We have." I then began to live the most intense thirty seconds of my whole life. The verdict was pronounced by the foreman in a strong, clear voice which filled the courtroom, "Not Guilty." . . .

The verdict was recorded upon the oath of the jury and thus was reached what we believe to be the end of the most dramatic court trial involving the fundamental rights of the Negro in his whole history in this country.

i. "Election by Terror in Florida," by Walter F. White, *New Republic*, January 12, 1921

"I want to register."

"All right, Jim, you can, but I want to tell you something. Some god damned black . . . is going to get killed yet about this voting business."

The questioner is a colored man in Orange County, Florida. The answer is from a registrar, white, of course. The Negro, cognizant of the sinister truth of the reply he had received, would probably decide that it was not particularly healthy for him to press his request. Thus, in many ways equally as flagrant, did the election of 1920 proceed in Florida and other southern states.

The Ku Klux Klan, of infamous post–Civil War memory, has been actively revived in the South. Its avowed purpose is to "keep the nigger in his place," and to maintain, at all costs, "white supremacy." In spite of vigorous denials on the part of its leaders, the branches of this organization have entered upon a campaign of terror that can result in nothing but serious clashes involving the loss of many lives and the destruction of much property. The recent elections brought into full play all of the fear that "white supremacy" would crumble if Negroes were allowed to vote, augmented by the belief that the recent war experiences of the Negro soldier had made him less tractable than before. In many southern cities and towns, parades of the Klan were extensively advertised in advance and held on the night of October 30th, the Saturday before the election. The effect of these outturnings of robed figures, clad in the white hoods and gowns adorned with flaming red crosses, was probably astounding to those who believed in the efficacy of such methods. The principal danger to America of anarchistic organizations like the Klan lies in their distorted perspective of conditions. The Negro emerged from slavery ignorant, uneducated, superstitious. It was a simple task to terrify him by the sight of a band of men, clothed in white coming down a lonely road on a moonlight night. Today the Negro is neither so poor nor so ignorant, nor so easily terrified, a fact known to everybody but the revivers of the Ku Klux Klan. Instead of running to cover, frightened, his mood now is to protect himself and his family by fighting to the death. It is as though one attempted to frighten a man of forty by threatening him with some of the tales used to quiet him when he was an infant. The method just doesn't work. . . .

More serious and more distressing, however, was the situation found in Orange County where the election clash at Ocoee occurred. News dispatches of November 4th told of the killing of six colored men, one by lynching, and of two white men, when Mose Norman, a colored man, attempted to vote although he had not registered nor paid his poll tax. The facts, secured on the spot, reveal an entirely different story. Three weeks prior to the election, the local Ku Klux Klan sent word to the colored people of Orange County that no Negroes would be allowed to vote and that if any Negro tried to do so, trouble could be expected. Norman refused to be intimidated. The registration books of Orlando showed that he had qualified and registered. He was unpopular with the whites because he was too prosperous—he owned an orange grove for which he had refused offers of $10,000 several times. The prevailing sentiment was that Norman was too prosperous "for a nigger." When Norman went to the polls he was overpowered, securely beaten [and] his gun taken away from him. . . . A mob formed, went out and surrounded the colored settlement, applied kerosene, burned twenty houses, two churches, a school-house and a lodge hall. [A man named] Perry and the other beleaguered Negroes fought desperately. Two members of the mob were killed and two were wounded. Perry, with his arm shot away, was taken to Orlando and placed in jail. Shortly afterward, a detachment of the mob went to the county jail at Orlando, to which the sheriff voluntarily turned over the keys. The mob took Perry just outside the city and, more dead than alive, lynched him.

In the meantime, the colored men, women and children trapped in the burning houses fought desperately against insurmountable odds. Negroes attempting to flee were either shot down or forced back into the flames. The number killed will never be known. I asked a white citizen of Ocoee who boasted of his participation in the slaughter how many Negroes died. He declared that fifty-six were known to have been killed—that he had killed seventeen "niggers" himself. Almost before the embers had died down, eager souvenir hunters searched like vultures with ghoulish glee among the ruins for the charred bones of the hapless victims. The effect upon the adult white citizens was distressing enough—an air of meritorious work well done—but more appalling was the attitude of the children of the country. When asked about the rioting, an eleven year old white girl, intelligent and alert, told exultingly of "the fun we had when some niggers were burned up." The outlook for a more enlightened generation to come is indeed unpromising when a little girl can exhibit so callous an attitude toward such a revolting crime. . . .

What is the remedy? The United States Supreme Court has declared unconstitutional laws providing for the punishment of persons who by threats of violence have prevented citizens from voting. But there are two definite steps which can be taken. First, a complete and exhaustive Congressional investigation of the elections of 1920 should be made. Second, under the provisions of section 19 of Chapter 3 of the Federal Criminal Code due punishment should be meted out to those persons who committed the crimes referred to above and the many more which a real Congressional investigation would disclose. . . .

The tense feeling now existing indicates that definite action must be taken at an early date to correct the monstrous evils underlying the race problem. Unless they are taken, it is not at all improbable that our race riots have just begun.

j. U.S. Supreme Court, *Nixon v. Herndon, 273 U.S. 536 (1927)*

273 U.S. 536
NIXON
v.
HERNDON et al.
No. 117.
Argued and Submitted January 4, 1927.
Decided March 7, 1927.

Messrs. Louis Marshall, of New York City, F. C. Knollenberg, of El Paso, Tex., A. B. Spingarn, of New York City, R. J. Channell, of El Paso, Tex., Moorfield Storey, of Boston, Mass., and James A. Cobb, of Washington, D. C., for plaintiff in error. [273 U.S. 536, 537] Messrs. Claude Pollard and D. A. Simmons, both of Austin, Tex., for defendants in error. [273 U.S. 536, 539]

Mr. Justice HOLMES delivered the opinion of the Court.

This is an action against the Judges of Elections for refusing to permit the plaintiff to vote at a primary election in Texas. It lays the damages at five thousand dollars. The petition alleges that the plaintiff is a negro, a citizen of the United States and of Texas and a resident of El Paso, and in every way qualified to vote, as set forth in detail, except that the statute to be mentioned interferes with his right; that on July 26, 1924, a primary election was held at El Paso for the nomination of candidates for a senator and representatives in Congress and State and other offices, upon the Democratic ticket; that [273 U.S. 536, 540] the plaintiff, being a member of the Democratic party, sought to vote but was denied the right by defendants; that the denial was based upon a statute of Texas enacted in May, 1923 (Acts 38th Leg. 2d Called Sess. (1923) c. 32, 1 (Vernon's Ann. Civ. St. 1925, art. 3107)), and designated article 3093a, by the words of which "in no event shall a negro be eligible to participate in a Democratic party primary election held in the State of Texas," etc., and that this statute is contrary to the Fourteenth and Fifteenth Amendments to the Constitution of the United States. The defendants moved to dismiss upon the ground that the subject-matter of the suit was political and not within the jurisdiction of the Court and that no violation of the Amendments was shown. The suit was dismissed and a writ of error was taken directly to this Court. Here no argument was made on behalf of the defendants but a brief was allowed to be filed by the Attorney General of the State.

The objection that the subject-matter of the suit is political is little more than a play upon words. Of course the petition concerns political action but it alleges and seeks to recover for private damage. That private damage may be caused by such political action and may be recovered for in suit at law hardly has been doubted for over two hundred years, since *Ashby v. White*, 2 Ld. Raym. 938, 3 Ld. Raym. 320, and has been recognized by this Court. *Wiley v. Sinkler*, 179 U.S. 58, 64, 65 S., 21 S. Ct. 17; *Giles v. Harris*, 189 U.S. 475, 485, 23 S. Ct. 639. See also Judicial Code, 24(11), (12), (14); Act of March 3, 1911, c. 231; 36 Stat. 1087, 1092 (Comp. St. 991). If the defendants' conduct was a wrong to the plaintiff, the same reasons that allow a recovery for denying the plaintiff a vote at a final election allow it for denying a vote at the primary election that may determine the final result.

The important question is whether the statute can be sustained. But although we state it as a question, the answer does not seem to us open to a doubt. We find it unnecessary to consider the Fifteenth Amendment, because it seems to us hard to imagine a more direct and obvious infringement of the Fourteenth [273 U.S. 536, 541]. That Amendment, while it applies to all, was passed, as we know, with a special intent to protect the blacks from discrimination against them. Slaughter House Cases, 16 Wall. 36; *Strauder v. West Virginia*, 100 U.S. 303. That Amendment "not only gave citizenship and the privileges of citizenship to persons of color, but it denied to any State the power to withhold from them the equal protection of the laws. . . . What is this but declaring that the law in the States shall be the same for the black as for the white; that all persons, whether colored or white, shall stand equal before the laws of the States, and, in regard to the colored race, for whose protection the amendment was primarily designed, that no discrimination shall be made against them by law because of their color?" Quoted from the last case in *Buchanan v. Warley*, 245 U.S. 60, 77, 38 S. Ct. 16, 19 (62 L. Ed. 149, L. R. A. 1918C, 210, Ann. Cas. 1918A, 1201). See *Yick Wo v. Hopkins*, 118 U.S. 356, 374, 6 S. Ct. 1064. The statute of Texas in the teeth of the prohibitions referred to assumes to forbid negroes to take part in a primary election the importance of which we have indicated, discriminating against them by the distinction of color alone. States may do a good deal of classifying that it is difficult to believe rational, but there are limits, and it is too clear for extended argument that color cannot be made the basis of a statutory classification affecting the right set up in this case.

Judgment reversed.

k. "America's Greatest Institution: The Ku Klux Klan," *Messenger*, April 1926, by a KLUXER

The Ku Klux Klan stands for the highest ideals in American civilization. Its membership includes native whites, Protestant, Gentile conservatives. Why do we say that it is the greatest institution? Well, it stands above the law and the law is supreme in our country. Whenever the law gets in our way we trample it beneath our feet. Then, it is composed of the greatest of everything. The white people are the greatest race, the Protestants have the "savingest" religion, the Gentiles laud it over the Jews, our white natives are superior to all foreigners.

The Ku Klux Klan is great because it keeps Negroes in their places. Some smart niggers don't like this and they are supported by their white friends. But who can complain about being kept in his place when nearly everybody is struggling to find his place in life. Moreover, most of these white people who stand with the "niggers" have got Negro blood in their veins. We discovered "nigger" blood in the veins of one of our late Presidents and put him on the defensive. [This refers to President Warren G. Harding.] As a result he gave the niggers nothing during his administration because he had to prove that all his black corpuscles had been segregated from the white ones.

White supremacy! What's wrong with that? Does anybody want to return to the dark ages? I suppose you folks have not realized the seriousness of the situation which confronts us. Think of what I saw the other day: When a rather white Negro filled out an application blank for a civil service job he answered two questions like this: 1. Race? Black 2. Color? White.

Again we ain't going to have no Jews around here. These Jews ain't got no business tryin' to get all the business. We can stop it if the Gentiles will not be so gentle with them. Just tar and feather them. . . .

America is a sporting country. Yet they ask us why they burn Negroes. Can you think of any greater sport than hunting birds, shooting squirrels and rabbits, or having a barbecue picnic? And ain't the hunting and barbecuing better in proportion as the game is bigger?

l. "To the World," *The Crisis*, November 1921 (Manifesto of the Second Pan-African Congress), by W. E. B. DuBois

The absolute equality of races—physical, political and social—is the founding stone of world peace and human advancement. No one denies great differences of gift, capacity and attainment among individuals of all races, but the voices of science, religion, and practical politics is one in denying the God-appointed existence of super-races, or of races naturally and inevitably and eternally inferior.

That in the vast range of time, one group should in its industrial technique, or social organization, or spiritual vision, lag a few hundred years behind another, or forge fitfully ahead, or come to differ decidedly in thought, deed and ideal, is proof of the essential richness and variety of human nature, rather than proof of the co-existence of demi-gods and apes in human form. The doctrine of racial equality does not interfere with individual liberty, rather, it fulfills it. And of all the various criteria by which masses of men have in the past been prejudged and classified, that of the color of the skin and texture of the hair, is surely the most adventitious and idiotic. . . .

The insidious and dishonorable propaganda, which, for selfish ends, so distorts and denies facts as to represent the advancement and development of certain races of men as impossible and undesirable, should be met with widespread dissemination of the truth. The experiment of making the Negro slave a free citizen in the United States is not a failure; the attempts at autonomous government in Haiti and Liberia are not proofs of the impossibility of self-government among black men; the experience of Spanish America does not prove that mulatto democracy will not eventually succeed there; the aspirations of Egypt and India are not successfully to be met by sneers at the capacity of darker races. . . .

If it be proven that absolute world segregation by group, color or historic affinity is best for the future, let the white race leave the dark world and the darker world will gladly leave the white. But the proposition is absurd. This is a world of men, of men whose likenesses far outweigh their differences; who mutually need each other in labor and thought and dream, but who can successfully have each other only on terms of equality, justice and mutual respect. They are the real and only peacemakers who work sincerely and peacefully to this end.

The beginning of wisdom in inter-racial contact is the establishment of political institutions among suppressed peoples. The habit of democracy must be made to encircle the earth. Despite the attempt that its practice is the secret and divine gift of the few, no habit is more natural or more widely spread among primitive people. . . . Local self-government with a minimum of help and oversight can be established tomorrow in Asia, in Africa, in America and in the Isles of the Sea. . . .

And this brings us to the crux of the matter: It is the shame of the world that today the relation between the main groups of mankind and their mutual estimate and respect is determined chiefly by the degree in which one can subject the other to its service, enslaving labor, making ignorance compulsory, uprooting ruthlessly religion and customs, and destroying government, so that the favored Few may luxuriate in the toil of the tortured Many. Science, Religion and Philanthropy have thus been made the slaves of world commerce and industry, and bodies, minds, souls of Fiji and Congo, are judged almost solely by the quotations on the Bourse. . . .

The Negro race through its thinking intelligentsia is demanding:

I—The recognition of civilized men as civilized despite their race or color

II—Local self government for backward groups, deliberately rising as experience and knowledge grow to complete self government under the limitations of a self governed world

III—Education in self knowledge, in scientific truth and in industrial technique, undivorced from the art of beauty

IV—Freedom in their own religion and social customs, and with the right to be different and non-conformist

V—Co-operation with the rest of the world in government, industry and art on the basis of Justice, Freedom and Peace

VI—The ancient common ownership of the land and its natural fruits and defense against the unrestrained greed of invested capital

VII—The establishment under the League of Nations of an international institution for the study of Negro problems

VIII—The establishment of an international section in the Labor bureau of the League of Nations, charged with the protection of native labor. . . .

Chapter 5: Expressions of Pride

The 1920s witnessed two movements asserting African American identity and pride. Both the Marcus Garvey movement and the Harlem Renaissance manifest the sense of enthusiasm that coursed through black communities of the North. For the first time in American history, large communities of free black people could express their hope, demands and anger in public assemblies. The sheer energy and optimism of these documents, poems, and stories is compelling.

Marcus Garvey was the most controversial black leader of the 1920s. In a 1924 editorial, W. E. B. DuBois attacked him as "A Lunatic or a Traitor" for criticizing civil rights activists and murdering a former colleague who exposed Garvey's financial machinations (document a). Writing from prison the following year, Garvey explained his nationalist principles in his newspaper, the *Negro World*. "African Fundamentalism" stresses the accomplishments of African civilization, as Garvey saw them, and the need for international race solidarity (document b).

The Harlem Renaissance produced writers of all literary forms, but the poets are best remembered today. West Indian immigrant poet Claude McKay captured the new militant attitude in verse (documents c and d). His poems are written using old-fashioned, conservative meter and rhyme schemes, but his attitude is uncompromising. James Weldon Johnson used Old Testament cadences in "The Creation," an excerpt from *God's Trombones* (document e). Among the novelists, Jessie Redmon Fauset wrote about African Americans who were the cultural equal of whites. In this excerpt from *Plum Bun*, the character Angela Murray is not "passing" for white but conducting her life without regard for the low expectations that white people have about her potential (document f).

Bessie Smith personified the blues in the 1920s. She was a big, imposing woman who lived life to the full and sang about her joys and sorrows in a powerful, resonant voice. Her lyrics came right out of her life experience and often had something to do with love, sex, desire, and infidelity (document g).

Sources

Marcus Garvey extract first printed in serial form, *Pittsburgh Courier*, 1930.

Claude McKay, "If We Must Die," *Liberator* 5 (May 1922): 16.

Claude McKay, "The White House," *Liberator* 2 (July 1919): 21.

W. E. B. DuBois, "A Lunatic or a Traitor," *The Crisis* (May 1924). The author wishes to thank the Crisis Publishing Company, the publisher of the magazine of the NAACP, for the use of this work.

James Weldon Johnson, "The Creation," in *God's Trombones*. New York: Viking Press, 1927. Copyright renewed in 1955 by Grace Nail Johnson. Used by permission of Viking Penguin, a division of Penguin Group (USA).

Jessie Redmon Fauset, *Plum Bun: A Novel without a Moral*. New York: Frederick A. Stokes Company, 1929.

Bessie Smith, "Please Help Me Get Him off My Mind." New York: Empress Music, 1928.

a. "A Lunatic or a Traitor," by W. E. B. DuBois, *The Crisis*, May 1924

In its endeavor to avoid any injustice toward Marcus Garvey and his followers, *The Crisis* has almost leaned backward. Notwithstanding his wanton squandering of hundreds of thousands of dollars we have refused to assume that he was a common thief. In spite of his monumental and persistent lying we have discussed only the larger and truer aspects of his propaganda. We have refrained from all comment on his trial and conviction for fraud. We have done this too in spite of his personal vituperation of the editor of *The Crisis* and persistent and unremitting repetition of falsehood after falsehood as to the editor's beliefs and acts and as to the program of the N.A.A.C.P.

In the face, however, of the unbelievable depths of debasement and humiliation to which this demagog has descended in order to keep himself out of jail, it is our duty to say openly and clearly:

Marcus Garvey is, without doubt, the most dangerous enemy of the Negro race in America and in the world. He is either a lunatic or a traitor. He is sending all over this country tons of letters and pamphlets appealing to Congressmen, business men, philanthropists and educators to join him on a platform whose half concealed planks may be interpreted as follows:

That no person of Negro descent can ever hope to become an American citizen.

That forcible separation of the races and the banishment of Negroes to Africa is the only solution of the Negro problem.

That race war is sure to follow any attempt to realize the program of the N.A.A.C.P.

We would have refused to believe that any man of Negro descent could have fathered such a propaganda if the evidence did not lie before us in black and white signed by this man. . . .

Not even Tom Dixon or Ben Tillman or the hatefulest enemies of the Negro have ever stooped to a more vicious campaign than Marcus Garvey, sane or insane, is carrying on. He is not attacking white prejudice, he is grovelling before it and applauding it; his only attack is on men of his own race who are striving for freedom; his only contempt is for Negroes; his only threats are for black blood. And this leads us to a few plain words:

1. No Negro in America ever had a fairer and more patient trial that Marcus Garvey. He convicted himself by his own admissions, his swagger-

ing monkey-shines in the court room with monocle and long tailed coat and insults to the judge and prosecuting attorney.

2. Marcus Garvey was long refused bail, not because of his color, but because of the repeated threats and cold blooded assaults charged against the organization. He himself openly threatened to "get" the District Attorney. The followers had repeatedly to be warned from intimidating witnesses and he was sent to jail therefor. One of his former trusted officials, after being put out of the Garvey organization, brought the long concealed cash account of the organization to this office and we published it. Within two weeks the man was shot in the back in New Orleans and killed. We know nothing of Garvey's personal connection with these cases but we do know that today his former representative lies in jail in Liberia sentenced to death for murder. The District Attorney believed that Garvey's "army" had arms and ammunition and was prepared to "shoot up" colored Harlem if he was released.

b. "African Fundamentalism," by Marcus Garvey, *Pittsburgh Courier*, 1930

Fellow Men of the Negro Race, Greeting:

The time has come for the Negro to forget and cast behind him his hero worship and adoration of other races, and to start out immediately, to create and emulate heroes of his own.

We must canonize our own saints, create our own martyrs, and elevate to positions of fame and honor black men and women who have made their distinct contributions to our racial history. Sojourner Truth is worthy of the place of sainthood alongside of Joan of Arc; Crispus Attucks and George William Gordon are entitled to the halo of martyrdom with no less glory than that of the martyrs of any other race. Toussaint L'Ouverture's brilliancy as a soldier and statesman outshone that of a Cromwell, Napoleon and Washington; hence, he is entitled to the highest place as a hero among men. Africa has produced countless numbers of men and women, in war and in peace, whose lustre and bravery outshine that of any other people. Then why not see good and perfection in ourselves?

Ours the Right to Our Doctrine

We must inspire a literature and promulgate a doctrine of our own without any apologies to the powers that be. The right is ours and God's. Let contrary sentiment and cross opinions go to the winds. Opposition to race independence is the weapon of the enemy to defeat the hopes of an unfortunate people. We are entitled to our own opinions and not obligated to or bound by the opinions of others.

A Peep at the Past

If others laugh at you, return the laughter to them; if they mimic you, return the compliment with equal force. They have no more right to dishonor, disrespect and disregard your feeling and manhood than you have in dealing with them. Honor them when they honor you; disrespect and disregard them when they vilely treat you. Their arrogance is but skin deep and an assumption that has no foundation in morals or in law. They have sprung from the same family tree of obscurity as we have; their history is as rude in its primitiveness as ours; their ancestors ran wild and naked, lived in caves and in the branches of trees, like monkeys, as ours; they made human sacrifices, ate the flesh of their own dead and the raw meat of the wild beast for centuries even as they accuse us of doing; their cannibalism was more prolonged than ours; when we were embracing the arts and sciences on the banks of the Nile their ancestors were still drinking human blood and eating out of the skulls of their conquered dead; when our civilization had reached the noonday of progress they were still running naked and sleeping in holes and caves with rats, bats and other insects and animals. After we had already unfathomed the mysteries of the stars and reduced the heavenly constellations to minute and regular calculus they were still backwoodsmen, living in ignorance and blatant darkness.

Why Be Discouraged?

The world today is indebted to us for the benefits of civilization. They stole our arts and sciences from Africa. Then why should we be ashamed of ourselves? Their MODERN IMPROVEMENTS are but DUPLICATES of a grander civilization that we reflected thousands of years ago, without the advantage of what is buried and still hidden, to be resurrected and reintroduced by the intelligence of our generation and our prosperity. Why should we be discouraged because somebody laughs at us today? Who is to tell what tomorrow will bring forth? Did they not laugh at Moses, Christ and Mohammed? Was there not a Carthage, Greece and Rome? We see and have changes every day, so pray, work, be steadfast and be not dismayed.

Nothing Must Kill the Empire Urge

As the Jew is held together by his RELIGION, the white races by the assumption and the unwritten law of SUPERIORITY, and the Mongolian by the precious tie of BLOOD, so likewise the Negro must be united in one GRAND RACIAL HIERARCHY. Our UNION MUST KNOW NO CLIME, BOUNDARY, or NATIONALITY. Like the great Church of Rome, Negroes the world over MUST PRACTICE ONE FAITH, that of Confidence in themselves, with One God! One Aim! One Destiny! Let no religious scruples, no political machination divide us, but let us hold together under all climes and in every country, making among ourselves a Racial Empire upon which "the sun shall never set."

Allegiance to Self First

Let no voice but your own speak to you from the depths. Let no influence but your own raise you in time of peace and time of war. Hear all, but attend only that which concerns you.

Your first allegiance shall be to your God, then to your family, race and country. Remember always that the Jew in his political and economic urge is always first a Jew; the white man is first a white man under all circumstances, and you can do no less than being first and always a Negro, and then all else will take care of itself. Let no one inoculate you for their own conveniences. There is no humanity before that which starts with yourself. "Charity begins at home." First to thyself be true, and "thou canst not then be false to any man."

We Are Arbiters of Our Own Destiny

God and Nature first made us what we are, and then out of our own creative genius we make ourselves what we want to be. Follow always that great law.

Let the sky and God be our limit, and Eternity our measurement. There is no height to which we cannot climb by using the active intelligence of our own minds. Mind creates, and as much as we desire in Nature we can have through the creation of our own minds. Being at present the scientifically weaker race, you shall treat others only as they treat you; but in your homes and everywhere possible you must teach the higher development of science to your children; and be sure to develop a race of scientists par excellence, for in science and religion lies our only hope to withstand the evil designs of modern materialism. Never forget your God. Remember, we live, work and pray for the establishing of a great and binding RACIAL HIERARCHY, the founding of a RACIAL EMPIRE whose only natural, spiritual and political limits shall be God and "Africa, at home and abroad."

MARCUS GARVEY

Source Notes

Printed in the *Negro World*, June 6, 1925, as a front-page editorial; written in the Atlanta Federal Penitentiary. Original headlines omitted. Creed reprinted in slightly revised form, under the title "African Fundamentalism," as a Universal Negro Improvement Association poster, sold by mail order through the *Negro World* by Amy Jacques Garvey, 1925.

c. "If We Must Die," by Claude McKay

> If we must die, let it not be like hogs
> Hunted and penned in an inglorious spot,
> While round us bark the mad and hungry dogs,
> Making their mock at our accursed lot.
> If we must die, O let us nobly die,
> So that our precious blood may not be shed
> In vain; then even the monsters we defy
> Shall be constrained to honor us though dead!
> O kinsmen! we must meet the common foe!
> Though far outnumbered let us show us brave,
> And for their thousand blows deal one deathblow!
> What though before us lies the open grave?
> Like men we'll face the murderous, cowardly pack,
> Pressed to the wall, dying, but fighting back!

d. "The White House," by Claude McKay

> Your door is shut against my tightened face,
> And I am sharp as steel with discontent;
> But I possess the courage and the grace
> To bear my anger proudly and unbent.
> The pavement slabs burn loose beneath my feet,
> A chafing savage, down the decent street;
> And passion rends my vitals as I pass,
> Where boldly shines your shattered door of glass.
> Oh, I must search for wisdom every hour,
> Deep in my wrathful bosom sore and raw,
> And find in it the superhuman power
> To hold me to the letter of your law!
> Oh, I must keep my heart inviolate
> Against the potent poison of your hate.

e. "The Creation: A Negro Sermon," by James Weldon Johnson (excerpt)

And God stepped out on space,
And He looked around and said,
"I'm lonely
I'll make me a world"

And as far as the eye of God could see
Darkness covered everything,
Blacker than a hundred midnights
Down in a cypress swamp.

Then God smiled,
And the light broke,
And the darkness rolled up on one side,
And the light stood shining on the other,
And God said, *"That's good!"*

Then God reached out and took the light in His hands,
And God rolled the light around in His hands
Until He made the sun;
And He set that sun a-blazing in the heavens.
And the light that was left from making the sun
God gathered it up in a shining ball
And flung it against the darkness,
Spangling the night with the moon and stars.
Then down between
The darkness and the light
He hurled the world;
And God said, *"That's good."*

Then God Himself stepped down—
And the sun was on His right hand
And the moon was on His left;
The stars were clustered about His head,
And the earth was under His feet.
And God walked, and where He trod
His footsteps hollowed the valleys out
And bulged the mountains up.

Then He stopped and looked, and saw
That the earth was hot and barren.
So God stepped over to the edge of the world
And He spat out the seven seas;
He batted His eyes, and the lightnings flashed;
He clapped His hands, and the thunders rolled;
And the waters above the earth came down,
The cooling waters came down.

f. Excerpt from *Plum Bun*, by Jessie Redmon Fauset

Angela took the sketch of Hetty Daniels to school. "What an interesting type!" said Gertrude Quale, the girl next to her. "Such cosmic and tragic unhappiness in that face. What is she, not an American?"

"Oh yes she is. She's an old coloured woman who's worked in our family for years and she was born right here in Philadelphia."

"Oh coloured! Well, of course I suppose you would call her an American though I never think of darkies as Americans. Coloured—yes that would account for that unhappiness in her face. I suppose they all mind it awfully."

It was the afternoon for the life class. The model came in, a short, rather slender young woman with a faintly pretty, shrewdish face full of a certain dark, mean character. Angela glanced at her thoughtfully, full of pleasant anticipation. She liked to work for character, preferred it even to beauty. The model caught her eye, looked away and again turned her full gaze upon her with an insistent, slightly incredulous stare. It was Esther Bayliss who had once been in the High School with Angela. She had left not long after Mary Hastings' return to her boarding school.

Angela saw no reason why she should speak to her and presently, engrossed in the portrayal of the round, yet pointed, little face, forgot the girl's identity. But Esther kept her eyes fixed on her former school-mate with a sort of intense, angry brooding so absorbing that she forgot her pose and Mr. Shields spoke to her two or three times. On the third occasion he said not unkindly, "You'll have to hold your pose better than this, Miss Bayliss, or we won't be able to keep you on."

"I don't want you to keep me on." She spoke with an amazing vindictiveness. "I haven't got to the point yet where I'm going to lower myself to pose for a coloured girl."

He looked around the room in amazement; no, Miss Henderson wasn't there, she never came to this class he remembered. "Well after that we couldn't keep you anyway. We're not taking orders from our models. But there's no coloured girl here."

"Oh yes there is, unless she's changed her name." She laughed spitefully. "Isn't that Angela Murray over there next to that Jew girl?" In spite of himself, Shields nodded. "Well, she's coloured though she wouldn't let you know. But I know. I went to school with her in North Philadelphia. And I tell you I wouldn't stay to pose for her not if you were to pay me ten times what I'm getting. Sitting there drawing from me just as though she were as good as a white girl!"

Astonished and disconcerted, he told his wife about it. "But I can't think she's really coloured, Mabel. Why she looks and acts just like a white girl. She dresses in better taste than anybody in the room. But that little wretch of a model insisted that she was coloured."

"Well she just can't be. Do you suppose I don't know a coloured woman when I see one? I can tell 'em a mile off."

g. From "Please Help Me Get Him off My Mind," by Bessie Smith

> I've cried and worried, all night I laid and groaned.
> I've cried and worried, all night I laid and groaned.
> I used to weigh two hundred now I'm down to skin and bones.
>
> It's all about a man who always kicked and dogged me 'round.
> It's all about a man who always kicked and dogged me 'round.
> And when I try to kill him that's when my love for him comes down.
>
> I've come to see you gypsy, beggin' on my bended knees,
> I've come to see you gypsy, beggin' on my bended knees,
> That man's put something on me, oh take it off of me, please.
>
> It starts at my forehead and goes clean down to my toes,
> It starts at my forehead and goes clean down to my toes,
> Oh, how I'm sufferin' gypsy, nobody but the good Lawd knows.
>
> Gypsy don't hurt him, fix him for me one more time,
> Oh, don't hurt him gypsy, fix him for me one more time,
> Just make him love me, but, please mam, take him off my mind.

Bibliographic Essay

This essay will orient the reader to the literature on this period. In much of it, the writers are trying to assess the evolving sentiments of the nation regarding race relations. I call attention only to books that I used, but there are many other very good books on all of these subjects. I also refer to some general reference works that do not focus on African American history.

Many outstanding primary sources illustrate the experience of the New Negroes of the 1920s. Some of the African American newspapers are on microfilm. The magazine of the NAACP, *The Crisis*, and the Urban League's *Opportunity* are both lively reading. Herbert Aptheker's *A Documentary History of the Negro People in the United States*, volume 3 (1973, reprinted 1993), contains many reports, letters, articles, and speeches from this period. The records of civil rights organizations such as the NAACP and the papers of prominent leaders show the challenges of the struggle against Jim Crow.

A growing literature describes the participation of African Americans in World War I. Theodore Kornweibel's *"Investigate Everything": Federal Efforts to Compel Black Loyalty during World War I* (2002) emphasizes African American indifference to the war effort, as well as federal repression of dissent. Emmett J. Scott, the black special assistant to the secretary of war, is decidedly patriotic in his *Official History of the American Negro in the World War* (1919, reprinted 1969). A first-hand account by two relief workers, Addie W. Hunton and Kathryn M. Johnson, *Two Colored Women with the American Expeditionary Forces*, ed. Adele Logan Alexander (1920, reprinted 1997), shows the mixed feelings of African American soldiers about the army.

The best general description of the "Red Summer" of 1919 remains Arthur I. Waskow's *From Race Riot to Sit-In, 1919 and the 1960s: A Study in the Connections between Conflict and Violence* (1967). William L. Tuttle's outstanding *Race Riot: Chicago in the Red Summer of 1919* (1970, reprinted 1996) gives a rounded picture of Chicago and shows how racial tensions increased over time. Scott Ellsworth's book on the Tulsa race riot, *Death in a Promised Land: The Tulsa Race Riot of 1921* (1982), sets the event in the wider context of antiradical violence. Richard C. Cortner in *A Mob Intent on Death: The NAACP and the Arkansas Riot Cases* (1988) focuses on the complicated legal history of the case and its implications. The less-known riots are usually described in community studies such as Constance McLaughlin Green's *The Secret City: A History of Race Relations in the Nation's Capital* (1967). A more focused look at the nation's capital is Jacqueline M. Moore, *Leading the Race: The Transformation of the Black Elite in the Nation's Capital, 1880–1920* (1999). NAACP leader Mary White Ovington mentions the Longview battle in her memoir, *The Walls Came Tumbling Down* (1969), and Walter White recalls his Arkansas experience in *A Man Called White* (1948).

There is an enormous literature on the Great Migration. The most important resource is still the 1935 report of the federal census. A useful overview of the entire process is Florette Henri's *Black Migration: Movement North, 1900–1920* (1975). A book of essays edited by Joe William Trotter, *The Great Migration in Historical Perspective: New Dimensions of Race, Class, and Gender* (1991), has an excellent bibliographic preface that traces the evolution of research. Important community studies include Gilbert Osofsky, *Harlem: The Making of a Ghetto, 1890–1930* (1963); Kenneth Kusmer, *A Ghetto Takes Shape: Black Cleveland, 1870–1930* (1976); Peter Gottlieb, *Making Their Own: Southern Blacks' Migration to Pittsburgh, 1916–1930* (1987); Joe William Trotter, *Black Milwaukee: The Making of an Industrial Proletariat, 1915–1945* (1988), and *Blacks in Southern West Virginia, 1915–1932* (1990); James R. Grossman, *Land of Hope: Chicago, Black Southerners and the Great Migration* (1989); Richard Walter Thomas, *Life for Us Is What We Make It: Building Black Community in Detroit, 1915–1945* (1999); and Quintard Taylor, *In Search of the Racial Frontier: African Americans in the American West, 1528–1990* (1999). Pete Daniel's *The Shadow of Slavery: Peonage in the South, 1901–1969* (1972) describes the persistence of black landlessness. A lot more remains to be written on the rural South in the 1920s.

Chapter 3 on community institutions relied especially on standard reference works. These include *Organizing Black America: An Encyclopedia of African American Associations*, ed. Nina Mjagkij (2001); *The Dictionary of American Negro Biography*, ed. Rayford Logan (1982); *Black Women in America: An Historical Encyclopedia*, eds. Darlene Clark Hine, Elsa Barkley Brown, and Rosalyn Terborg-Penn (1994); *African American Women: A Bio-*

graphical Dictionary, ed. Dorothy Salem (1993); *Notable Black American Women*, ed. Jessie Carney Smith (1992); and *The Encyclopedia of African American Culture and History*, eds. Jack Salzman, David L. Smith, and Cornel West (1996).

Particularly useful for an understanding of black religion is C. Eric Lincoln, *The Black Church in the African American Experience* (1990). The authoritative work on the YMCA is Nina Mjagkij, *Light in the Darkness: African Americans and the YMCA, 1852–1946* (1994); the Commission on Interracial Cooperation appears in that book. Also noteworthy is John Egerton's *Speak Now against the Day: The Generation before the Civil Rights Movement in the South* (1994), which focuses on the civil rights struggles of the 1930s and 1940s.

Juliet E. K. Walker provides a magnificent overview, with thorough detail, of African American business ventures in *The History of Black Business in America: Capitalism, Race, Entrepreneurship* (1998). Nancy J. Weiss's *The National Urban League, 1910–1940* (1974) gives a solid picture of that organization. Most books on labor in this period focus on the Brotherhood of Sleeping Car Porters, including Jervis Anderson's *A. Philip Randolph: A Biographical Portrait* (1972). Eric Arnesen's *Brotherhoods of Color: Black Railroad Workers and the Struggle for Equality* (2002) tells the little-known story of black workers in other railroad departments.

On African American women's struggles, see Darlene Clark Hine and Kathleen Thompson, *A Shining Thread of Hope: The History of Black Women in America* (1998), and Paula Giddings, *When and Where I Enter: The Impact of Black Women on Race and Sex in America* (1984), for general texts. Dorothy Salem, *To Better Our World: Black Women in Organized Reform, 1890–1920* (1990), and Roslyn Terborg-Penn, *African American Women in the Struggle for the Vote, 1850–1920* (1998), focus on activists.

In addition to reference works, the section on higher education and professional associations was derived from *The Crisis* and James D. Anderson's *The Education of Blacks in the South, 1860–1935* (1988). On the role of the black press, see Roi Ottley, *The Lonely Warrior: The Life and Times of Robert S. Abbott* (1955); Andrew Buni, *Robert L. Vann of the Pittsburgh Courier: Politics and Black Journalism* (1974); and Stephen R. Fox, *The Guardian of Boston: William Monroe Trotter* (1970).

Books on the civil rights movement include memoirs, biographies, studies of specific issues such as lynching, and general overviews of the period. Many of the 1920s-era NAACP leaders wrote memoirs. DuBois wrote three memoirs over the course of his long life. Especially helpful is *Dusk of Dawn*, the

1940 book that is closest to these events. James Weldon Johnson's beautifully written *Along This Way* (1933, reprinted 1968) recounts Johnson's early career and his efforts as NAACP leader in the 1920s. Walter White's *A Man Called White* (1948) is unreliable but gives the reader a good sense of the atmosphere in the association (the NAACP). Mary White Ovington wrote several memoirs that help bring the events of this period to life: *Black and White Sat Down Together: The Reminiscences of an NAACP Founder* (reissued 1995), *The Walls Came Tumbling Down* (originally published 1947, reissued 1969), and *Portraits in Color* (1927). Ovington encouraged female leaders in the association and offers some memorable portraits of them.

These leaders are now also the subjects of biographies. Several have been written about DuBois, but the outstanding work is by David Levering Lewis, who won the Pulitzer Prize both for *W. E. B. DuBois: Biography of a Race, 1869–1919* (1993) and *W. E. B. DuBois: The Fight for Equality and the American Century, 1919–1963* (2000). Manning Marable's *W. E. B. DuBois: Black Radical Democrat* (1986) offers a nuanced interpretation of DuBois's thought from a leftist point of view. Eugene Levy's *James Weldon Johnson: Black Leader, Black Voice* (1973) focuses on Johnson as NAACP leader. A recent biography of Johnson's assistant is *White: The Biography of Walter White, Mr. NAACP* by Kenneth Janken (2003). Carolyn Wedin's *Inheritors of the Spirit: Mary White Ovington and the Founding of the NAACP* (1997) puts the early civil rights movement in the context of the wider reform movement. For the association as a whole, see Charles Flint Kellogg, *The NAACP: A History of the National Association for the Advancement of Colored People, 1909–1920* (1969), and Mark Robert Schneider, *We Return Fighting: The Civil Rights Movement in the Jazz Age* (2002).

There are several good books on lynching and the struggle against it, including Robert L. Zangrando, *The NAACP Crusade against Lynching, 1909–1950* (1980), and Fitzhugh W. Brundage's *Lynching in the New South: Georgia and Virginia, 1880–1930* (1993), which analyzes the various types of lynchings. Claudine Ferrell discusses the constitutional issues involved in the Dyer bill in *Nightmare and Dream: Anti-Lynching in Congress, 1917–1922* (1986). Monte Akers has written a chilling study of the Kirvin burnings at the stake in *Flames after Midnight: Murder, Vengeance and the Desolation of a Texas Community* (1999).

On the initial strategy for overthrowing segregation in education, see Mark Tushnet, *The NAACP's Legal Strategy against Segregation in Education, 1925–1950* (1987). The Gary, Indiana, struggle appears in James B. Lane's *City of the Century: A History of Gary, Indiana* (1978). August Meier and

Elliott Rudwick describe the Springfield, Ohio, school boycott in "Early Boycotts of Segregated Schools: The Case of Springfield, Ohio," in *American Quarterly* 20, no. 4 (1968). On the Kentucky executions, see George C. Wright, *Racial Violence in Kentucky, 1865–1940: Lynchings, Mob Rule, and "Legal Lynchings"* (1990). For use of the death penalty, see David Lester, *The Death Penalty: Issues and Answers, 1608–1985* (1998). An excellent monograph on the Houston events of 1917 is Robert V. Haynes, *A Night of Violence: The Houston Riot of 1917* (1976). For the Pan-African Congresses, see *The Crisis* for first-hand reporting and the DuBois memoirs and biographies.

The fight against the white primary is recorded in Darlene Clark Hine, *Black Victory: The NAACP and the Destruction of the Democratic White Primary, 1924–1944* (1979), and Conrey Bryson, *Dr. Lawrence A. Nixon and the White Primary* (1974, reprinted 1992). On the Ku Klux Klan, see Kenneth T. Jackson, *The Ku Klux Klan in the City, 1915–1930* (1967, reprinted 1992), which argues that Klansmen were mostly urban Protestants alarmed by the growing political power of Catholics. Charles C. Alexander, *The Ku Klux Klan in the Southwest* (1965, reprinted 1995), David C. Chalmers, *Hooded Americanism: the History of the Ku Klux Klan* (1987), and Richard E. Tucker, *The Dragon and the Cross: The Rise and Fall of the Ku Klux Klan in Middle America* (1991), round out the picture.

On black politics in the 1920s, see August Meier's *Negro Thought in America, 1880–1915* (1963). *Politics in Black America: Crisis and Change in the Negro Ghetto* (1973), ed. Martin Kilson, reveals the "patron-client" relationship between party bosses and black community leaders. For more on Chicago and Oscar de Priest, see Christopher Reed, *The Chicago NAACP and the Rise of Black Political Leadership* (1998).

Marcus Garvey is the subject of several biographies and analyses of his work. E. David Cronon's biography, *Black Moses: The Story of Marcus Garvey and the Universal Negro Improvement Association* (1955, reprinted 1969), is generally enthusiastic about Garvey's encouragement of pride. Judith Stein, in *The World of Marcus Garvey: Race and Class in Modern Society* (1986), discusses Garvey's politics and the social history of the movement. Robert A. Hill offers useful commentary as editor of *Marcus Garvey and the Universal Negro Improvement Association Papers* (1983).

The largest body of literature focuses on the Harlem Renaissance. An essential book is David Levering Lewis's *When Harlem Was in Vogue* (1979), which appreciates the verve of the Harlem writers but casts a sober eye on their achievement. Lewis also edited an anthology, *The Portable Harlem Renaissance Reader* (1994). George Hutchinson's *The Harlem Renaissance in*

Black and White (1995) argues that white New York radicals provided an important context for the literary movement. Alain Locke edited the classic anthology of the new writers in 1925, *The New Negro: Voices of the Harlem Renaissance*. In addition, there is a volume on African American writers in *The Dictionary of Literary Biography*, volume 51 (1987). All the major writers and many of the less known ones are the subjects of biographies or literary analyses. Many of the novels of the period are still in print. It would take too many pages to list the studies on just the leading writers who appear in this text.

There is also a good selection of books on jazz during this time. Particularly useful is *Jazz Masters of the 1920s*, by Richard Hadlock (1972), and Lewis Porter and Michael Ullman's *Jazz: From Its Origins to the Present* (1992). For the Broadway musicals, James Weldon Johnson's *Black Manhattan* (1930) is still a classic. On baseball, see *The Biographical Encyclopedia of the Negro Baseball Leagues*, by James A. Riley (1994).

Index

About the Author

Mark Robert Schneider is the author of *Boston Confronts Jim Crow* (1997) and *We Return Fighting: The Civil Rights Movement in the Jazz Age* (2001). He is adjunct instructor of History at Tufts University and Suffolk University.